Japan
a working holiday guide

Louise Southerden

Global Exchange
Newcastle

Japan: a working holiday guide

First published 1997
This second edition 2001

Published by
Global Exchange Pty Ltd (ABN 66 006 887 556)
PO Box 852
Newcastle NSW 2300
Australia
Tel: (02) 4929 4688
Fax: (02) 4929 4727
Email: info@globalexchange.com.au
Web: www.globalexchange.com.au

Cover design by Rob Thom Design, Melbourne, from a photograph of a temple roof in Kyoto by the author.
Page design and layout by Anna Kaemmerling, Global Exchange, Newcastle.
Printed in Australia by Australian Print Group, Maryborough.

Copyright © Global Exchange

All rights reserved. This book is copyright. Apart from any fair dealings for the purpose of private study, criticism, research or review as permitted under the Copyright Act (Australia), no part may be reproduced by any process without written permission. Enquiries should be addressed to the publisher at the above address. Thank you.

National Library of Australia
Cataloguing-in-Publication data:
Southerden, Louise, 1965-
Japan: a working holiday guide.

2nd ed.
Bibliography.
ISBN 1 876438 34 7

1. Temporary employment - Japan. 2. Employment in foreign countries. 3. Japan - Description and travel. 4. Japan - Social life and customs. I. Title.

915.204

Disclaimer

The author, publisher and their agents believe all information supplied in this guide to be correct at the time of printing. However, the parties are not in a position to provide a guarantee to this effect and accept no liability in the event of information proving incorrect. Opportunities, regulations, organisations and addresses change over time. This guide does not take the place of professional advice from travel agents, doctors and relevant others. The listing of organisations in this publication does not imply recommendation.

For Pete and Alda, for their true friendship, and my dad for his love and support.

Acknowledgements

Books are seldom the result of one person's efforts. This one wouldn't have been possible without several people: Bryan Havenhand for asking me to write the first edition in 1997. Stewart Clark for showing me the Japan he knew and translating everything before my Japanese was anywhere near passable. Friends in Japan and Australia who helped in both tangible and not so tangible ways: Mari and Hiroshi Narita, Maki Naganuma, Vince Panero, David MacKail, Kai Shinsaku, Kazue Morimoto, Miho Tanaka, Aiko Tsunesada, Mineo Oshiro, Sean Carey, Stephen McIntyre, my dad, Chris Buykx, Yasushi Nakano, Chie Tanaka, Aya Sato, Lourie Quirk and Janet Boyd. Alda Borror and Tete Moses for their longstanding, long distance friendships and for all the effort they put into helping me research this second edition. Rob Thom for his fantastic cover design. Lynley Aldridge at the Japan National Tourist Organisation, The Japan Foundation, Wendi Aylward at Exchange HQ, Gary Brown of the Japanese Language Institute and Mayu Kanamori for their contributions.

About the author

Louise Southerden is a writer, editor, photojournalist and surfer. Her articles and photographs have appeared in Australian and overseas publications and cover subjects as diverse as travelling by train in West Africa, hiking through Arnhem Land in northern Australia, surfing in Tasmania and, since 1992, various aspects of life and culture in Japan. In between writing and travelling, Louise obtained an honours degree in psychology and now applies her insights to her work as editor of *Waves SurfGirl*, an Australian surfing magazine. She first went to Japan in 1992 and still thinks of Miyazaki, located on the scenic coastline of southern Kyushu, as her 'second home'.

Contents

Introduction 6
Why Japan? 7
   Reasons to go 7
   How the Japanese view us 10
   Still have doubts? 11
Look before leaping 15
   The country 15
   A brief history of Japan 19
   Culture shock 25
   On being a *gaijin* 26
   Coping with the culture 27
   Crossing the language barrier 39
   A checklist of things to do and take 43
Arriving 48
   Changing money 48
   The Tourist Information Centre 49
   Getting out of the airport 50
First things first 54
   Exploring 54
   JAWHM 60
   Street addresses 61
   Police 62
   Alien registration 63
   Phones 64
   Post offices 66
   Money matters 68
   Name stamp 69
Living 70
   Japan — where the living is easy 70
   English language media 73
   Deciding where to live 76
   Accommodation options 78
   Where to look for accommodation 81
   A typical apartment 81

Keeping in touch	84
Furnishing your apartment	86
Shopping	89
Health	92
A day in the life of a Tokyo alien	95
Life as a rural alien	97
Working	99
Are there still jobs in Japan?	99
Visas and programs	100
Where to start	107
Teaching English	110
Non-teaching jobs	126
Hostessing	127
Hosting	133
Bar work	134
Modelling	136
Events work and acting	138
Jobs in the hospitality industry	138
Translating and interpreting	141
Professional jobs	144
Now for something completely different: odd jobs	146
Taking it to the streets	148
Sushi* and *sake	149
Gaijin food	149
Visiting someone's home for dinner	150
Eating etiquette	151
Japanese fast food	153
Some common Japanese dishes	155
Eating out	158
Drinking	161
What to drink	162
Where to drink	163
In search of the 'real' Japan	165
Top 12 'real' Japan experiences	165
A few more 'must do's'	178
Leaving	179
Appendix	181

Introduction

When I first went to Japan I was sure I could never live there. Out my aeroplane window Osaka was so daunting: grey apartment blocks and skyscrapers, even a grey ocean, and a reddy brown sunset that indicates there's too much pollution in the air. Kansai airport—spotlessly clean and orderly, with people dressed as uniformly as dolls and groups of Japanese tourists sheepishly tagging along behind a flag-toting guide—wasn't much more inviting. However, I'm grateful I didn't trust those first impressions. I'm glad I stayed long enough to be able to see beneath Japan's quirkiness.

And so this book is intended as a friend: one who will encourage you to venture forth. It will help with your preparations, be with you on the flight whispering last minute reassurances, and give you clues about what to do when you arrive. At the same time it acknowledges that part of travelling and being in a foreign country is about discovering things for yourself and feeling the foreignness first hand and learning to deal with it and even love it.

When I first went to Japan I had a few safety nets in place. I travelled with a Japanese-speaking friend, we had use of a car and accommodation was organised. It was only after I started my working holiday two years later, that I realised how much there is to know and what a scary place Japan can be for first-timers.

I ended up living mostly in Miyazaki, a city of 300,000, on one of the most scenic coastlines in Kysuhu. I now realise these were two of the best years of my life.

Although two years isn't a long time—and I don't pretend to be a 'Japan expert' by any means—it was long enough for me to learn some valuable lessons that I can pass on to newcomers, and short enough to ensure I hadn't become too 'Japanified' or forgotten what it's like to be one of those newcomers.

As they say in Japan before any leap into the unknown: *Gambatte*! ('Good luck' and 'Do your best!')

Why Japan?

Although I'd always wanted to live in a foreign country, my two-year working holiday in Japan happened virtually by chance. I hadn't studied Japanese at school, I didn't have any particular interest in things Japanese, in fact my knowledge of Japan and its culture was pretty limited. I wanted a change of pace and, like everyone, had heard about people teaching English in Japan, working minimal hours and making good money. I was eligible for a Japanese working holiday visa and so I went. Looking back on it now it all seems fairly straightforward, but at the time I was racked with all the doubts and anxieties that accompany any move away from familiar ground.

Living in Japan has changed how I think about the world and my place in it, how I see myself and what I value in life. I left full-time work in Sydney to live amidst rice paddies on the outskirts of Miyazaki, a coastal city in southern Kyushu. I worked for maybe 14 hours per week, which brought in enough money to live on, and the rest of the time I wrote, took pictures, surfed and hung out with my new friends. It was, to me, an idyllic, simple existence. There were other advantages, like experiencing an Asian culture first hand and living day-to-day in a foreign language, allowing it to seep in in a natural way. And I can now say that throughout all this I've gained some understanding of one of the most misunderstood countries on the planet.

That's my story, but there are as many 'living in Japan' stories as there are people to tell them. One way to decide if you're interested in living in a foreign country is to talk to those who already have. To start you thinking, here are a few impressions from *gaijin* who've lived in Japan.

Reasons to go

Why experience life only in Australia? We're so lucky, in the age we live in, we can go overseas and experience different lifestyles. You always

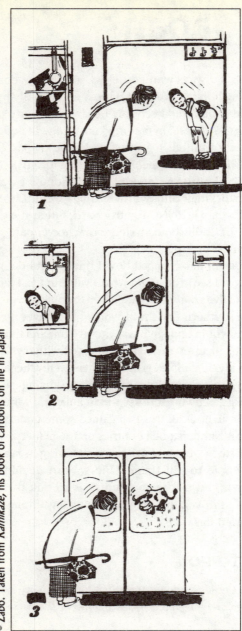

© Zabo. Taken from *Kamikaze*, his book of cartoons on life in Japan

come back a different person for that. If you're adaptable and accepting of different cultures, you can't help but gain from the experience. Jess Halford, working holiday maker from Sydney.

After almost eight months [living in Japan] I'm still not used to working only four hours a day. There's so much free time and if you're motivated you can fit a lot of things into your day and still lead a pretty cruisey existence. I didn't go for the money, and working only twenty hours a week I wasn't going to make a truckload anyway. However it's definitely enough to get by on depending how exorbitant your expenses are with the likes of going out every night, which is ridiculously easy to do. Andrew Quirk, working holiday maker from Dunedin, New Zealand.

I went there originally to make a bit of money, but also to have the experience ... I think everyone goes through waves of love and hate in Japan ... everything seems great one day and the next it sucks completely. I don't know anyone who's gone there and hasn't found work. Japan doesn't have to be expensive, my apartment was about ¥40,000 a month but I conducted lessons there so it paid for itself. If you're a high maintenance sort of person who needs a lot of support and friendships, you can get that from the foreign community no problem, but to the extent that you can and you feel capable and have the desire to mix with the local people, I think that's pretty valuable. Stewart Clark, an Australian who now lives permanently in Japan.

I'd studied Japanese at high school so it seemed a natural step to go to Japan on a working holiday. Living in Japan changed my outlook on many things as it was so different to anything I'd experienced before. I became more independent, in a sense it forced me to take responsibility for myself and my actions. When I came back to Australia I found work using my Japanese and assisting Japanese coming to Australia on a working holiday. Having been in that situation I realise now how important it is to have some assistance, and a place to go for advice. It has been interesting watching it from the other side of the coin. Even now I sometimes look at a tourist [in Sydney] and see myself lost in the middle of Tokyo. Wendi Aylward, who now manages Exchange HQ, a resource centre for working holiday makers in Sydney run by Council Exchanges.

I gained a sense of independence, of being able to strike out on my own in a country that's obviously very different from mine. As far as coming to a totally different culture, Japan is probably one of the most affable countries in the world. Japanese people are so non-confrontational. They themselves tend to lead their own people around and make sure everybody's taken care of, to the point where they explain to you things like 'The train is coming to a stop now, please be careful not to be jolted forward!' Every little detail is taken care of. It tends to belie your fears a lot. People bend over backwards to help you. Can you imagine being in America and apologising to a Japanese person because you couldn't speak Japanese to them? And yet that's what they do here in Japan: they apologise to foreigners for not being able to speak English. It's such an easy place to be. Peter Moses, an American who has been living in Japan for ten years.

I've learned that in Japan, kindness will come out of nowhere and slap you silly. As well as people staring at you because you're a foreigner and other stuff, compared to any other country in the world it's a piece of cake to live here. You overestimate the effects of culture shock in the beginning, and you underestimate the long-term effects [Japan can have] on you. Vince Panero, an American who lived in Japan for five years.

How the Japanese view us

Japanese perceptions of other countries vary, with young people usually better informed than their older relatives. Overall, they tend to know more about the US and even the UK (thanks to the influx of films and advertising from those countries) than about Canada, Australia or New Zealand. It's not uncommon, for instance, to have to explain that the seasons are reversed 'down under' compared to the northern hemisphere. This means that being in Japan is a two-way learning street and you can give as much as you receive. To illustrate this, I asked a few Japanese friends what they feel they've gained from interacting with the *gaijin* in their midst.

Japan is an isolated country in many ways, its culture is very strong, and as a result most Japanese think foreigners come from another world, another planet. Japanese have an inferiority complex about foreigners because foreigners look cool, and so on. When I was a university student I was like a stone in front of the foreign teachers, I couldn't talk to them. But since I've met more foreigners and been to Australia, I've changed my attitude. I think now we're not so different. There are some differences though, good things.

Foreign people can express themselves very clearly and they're very warm. When they scold a child, for instance, they hug the child afterwards, but Japanese people don't. I think it's good for foreigners to come to Japan because it's becoming more normal to communicate with them. In a few years it's even going to be compulsory for Japanese elementary [primary] school students to study English. Kazue Morimoto, an English conversation student.

I like the way foreigners think. Meeting my foreign friends and meeting my Japanese friends is so different. The Japanese I know all talk about their work, their companies, they don't seem to think about life as a whole. Whereas the foreigners I know give me advice about my life, and we talk about life a lot. Aiko Tsunesada, an English language teacher.

It's easier to work with foreigners than with Japanese. The foreigners I've worked with have a sense of responsibility towards their jobs. And as far as different nationalities, the Australians I've met have a nice relaxed manner, they're easy to work with. Not shy, not noisy, they're interested in other countries, they don't just want to speak about Australia all the time and they don't shout like some Americans I've met! And the New Zealanders I know always work hard and play hard. Mari Narita, an English language teacher.

If I only spoke Japanese, I'd only know about Japanese culture. Learning English helps me get to know other people, it's all about communicating with other people. Also Japanese people always call me either Tanaka's wife or Shuntaro's mother. No-one calls me Miho, but foreigners always call me Miho. They treat me as an individual. I really like that. Miho Tanaka, an English conversation student.

Still have doubts?

There will always be reasons why you shouldn't, couldn't or wouldn't go to Japan and it's true that Japan doesn't suit everyone. There are people who go, decide they don't like it and jump on the first plane home, but this can happen in any country. Then again if you're reading this book, chances are you have at least some interest in going there and maybe that alone will see you through at least until you realise you love it there! Now about those doubts ...

Isn't it expensive to live in Japan? The short answer is: it can be, but need not be. If you want to eat Western food, live in a Western-style apartment and hang out in Western bars and clubs, then you may as well be working back home for all the money you'll save, not to mention the cultural experiences you'll miss out on. Admittedly the prices for some things can be exorbitant—as my friend Pete Moses once said, 'A watermelon for $25! You don't want to eat it, you want to frame it!' For some details on current costs in Japan, mostly Tokyo, visit some of the websites mentioned in this book but also see www.thomascook.co.uk and www.timeout.com. For current exchange rates visit www.xe.net/ucc/ or www.oanda.com.

The trick is to live as the locals do. Japanese food is healthy and reasonably priced, and living conditions can be simple: you don't need much furniture in a Japanese-style apartment when all your living's done on the floor. It doesn't mean you have to become Japanese—you'd be hard pressed to pull that off anyway—but you can eat and live well on say, ¥2000 a day. Remember, if you're spending dollars or pounds in Japan it can become expensive because of the exchange rates, but once you start earning yen you'll be set. And for those working full-time in Japan: income tax is only seven per cent! Also, many employers, particularly large English conversation schools, pay for your transport to and from work, find affordable accommodation for you and sometimes assist with other expenses.

Don't I need to speak Japanese to work and live there?
When I arrived in Japan I didn't speak a word of Japanese, but within a month I was working and even had a few Japanese friends. You don't need to speak Japanese to teach English, which is what most *gaijin* do, although for some jobs (e.g. in ski resorts) the more Japanese you know the better will be the jobs you'll get (and the more you'll be able to negotiate better fees and working conditions). And don't rule out the possibility of learning to speak Japanese whilst you're there: while reading and writing Japanese can take years to master, conversational Japanese is easier than many other languages. Besides, when you're living in that language on a daily basis it's even easier.

In the meantime, however, it's reassuring to know that Japan caters for English-speaking foreigners like nowhere else. There are

English signs everywhere and English language movies, books and newspapers. You'll also find plenty of people wanting to speak to you in English, especially in the cities, and there are always other *gaijin* around when you do get homesick for a little 'real' English conversation.

But I don't know anyone in Japan. Japan is one of the easiest places I know to make friends. When I first arrived in Miyazaki I didn't know a soul but within a few days I'd met Pete, an American, who told me that he and most of the other *gaijin* living there already knew I'd arrived and was looking for work! Sometimes you might feel there are no secrets in expatriate communities, particularly those in small cities or towns. This, however, can be a good thing; it makes meeting people easy, which makes finding work and a place to live easy too. Most *gaijin* can remember what it was like to be new in Japan and not know anyone (or anything!), so they tend to look out for other newcomers.

It's not even that difficult to make friends with the locals, since many Japanese speak English and are eager to meet and talk with *gaijin* (and not always to practise their English). Even if they don't speak English, most Japanese are at least curious about foreigners and open to meeting new ones, and it never ceases to amaze me how well people of different cultures can communicate without the aid of a common language.

I'm not a teacher! Before I went to Japan I'd never taught anyone anything. Fortunately, prior experience is not a prerequisite for teaching English in Japan. Teaching jobs in Japan generally require minimal lesson preparation, little knowledge of English grammar or spelling, and little of the student management skills we usually associate with teaching. It's more important that you have a pleasant manner, an interest in people, plenty of patience (to wait for nervous students to reply to seemingly easy questions) and compassion (to understand that they're doing their best given the nature of their society and the pressures they are under).

I don't want to work 18-hour days like the Japanese. You'll be happy to hear that a working holiday visa only allows you to work 20 hours a week and most full-time teaching jobs in Japan (i.e.

if you're on a work visa) involve 25 to 30 hours a week. That said, many *gaijin* choose to supplement their incomes with a little 'unofficial' overtime by teaching private students (even if they're not working as an English teacher during the day). But even if you do land a job working for a Japanese company, chances are you won't be expected to slave away like your Japanese colleagues, because *gaijin* tend to dwell in an outsiders' zone, free of certain expectations and social rules.

I don't want to live in Tokyo or Osaka. Just because 75% of Japan's population lives in the metropolises on the Kanto plain (Tokyo, Yokohama, Kawasaki) and around Kansai (Osaka, Kobe, Kyoto), doesn't mean you have to live there too. There are plenty of smaller cities, towns and villages scattered throughout Japan for the urban-weary *gaijin*. Sure, most of the highly paid jobs are in the larger cities, but there's still a need for English speakers in smaller cities and towns. Even if you want to work in a big city it's still possible to live on the outskirts—amidst mountains or by the coast—but within a 40 minute train ride of work.

What will my friends back home say? Just as most Japanese don't know a lot about other countries, many of our countrymen (and women) don't know much about Japan beyond the stereotype of overworked salary men living in capsules and working in overcrowded bustling megacities. When I returned to Australia after living in Japan I felt like an unpaid diplomat, doing my bit for international relations by answering friends' questions about how I could live and, more to the point, *enjoy* living in Japan of all places!

There are certain segments of society within our home countries that hold rather negative attitudes to the Japanese and it's just as well to be prepared for them. There are those who focus on Japan's environmental record which has been tarnished by activities such as whaling, logging and the use of driftnets. There's the entire generation who fought against the Japanese in the Second World War and still regard all Japanese people with suspicion at best. Perhaps the most effective way to deal with all these attitudes is simply to be aware of them and remember that most of the people you'll meet in Japan will be as far removed from all these events as you.

Look before leaping

It's no secret that having some knowledge of a country before stepping off the plane—its history, the lie of the land, its climate and people—gives you a head start every time. For a country as old as Japan, with its mix of ancient traditions and high-tech modernity, this is particularly true. Following is a very brief tour through Japan's landscape, key historical events, culture and language.

The country

One of the most surprising things about Japan when you first see it on a map is its size, since a population of 127 million people can make any country look small. In fact Japan's land mass is as long as Australia's is wide and stretches for more than 3000 km from icy north to tropical south, crossing several climatic zones along the way.

There are four main islands: Honshu, Hokkaido, Shikoku and Kyushu, along with more than 3000 smaller islands, of which Okinawa is the most populated. Honshu is the main island, where most of those 127 million people live on the thin coastal strip between Tokyo and Osaka. Hokkaido, the northernmost island, is largely wilderness with some world class ski resorts and hiking trails. Shikoku is the small rural island just south of Honshu; it's also shaped like Australia, which is why some Japanese call Australia 'big Shikoku'. Kyushu is the southernmost of the big four and has the mildest climate.

Japan's natural elements, although seemingly taking a back seat to such an enormous human population, still have a significant influence on daily life. Apart from climatic extremes—climatically Japan extends from far north Queensland to the southern tip of New Zealand—the country is frequently at the mercy of earthquakes, volcanoes and *tsunami* (tidal waves). Japan's weather comes from the south, thanks to typhoons and tropical storms born in the equatorial zone, and from China's vast land mass to the west. Wherever you decide to live, you'll experience Japan's famous and

16 Japan: a working holiday guide

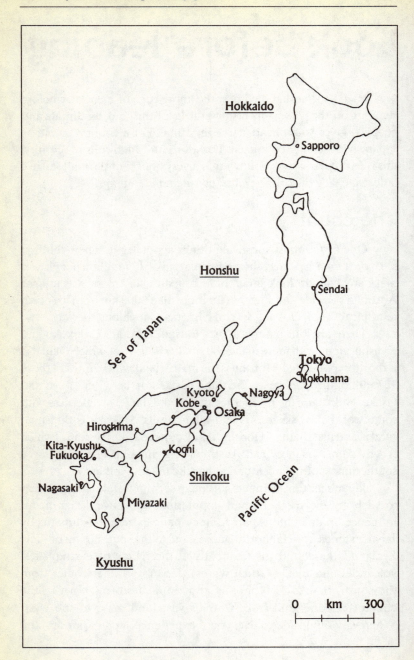

distinct four seasons, as well as the dreaded rainy season which is usually from mid-May to mid-June, and the typhoon season, usually from July to October. Summer is generally hot (around 32°C) and humid, winters are cold (particularly as so few houses are insulated) and it snows north of Tokyo. Remember we're talking Northern Hemisphere seasons: February is the most wintry month while July and August are the most steamy. Late spring (April–May) brings the cherry blossoms, they bloom in a front that travels from south to north up the length of the country. Autumn (September–November) brings another front, but from north to south as the landscape transforms again with the reds and yellows of the changing leaves.

You don't have to look very far to find evidence that Japan is one of the most geologically volatile countries in the world, boasting some 186 volcanoes of which more than 60 are active. Some, like Sakurajima in Kyushu, spew ash and volcanic dust into the air above their neighbouring cities so regularly that residents carry umbrellas whenever they go outdoors. There are about 1000 earthquakes in Japan every year, most too small to notice, serving only as a reminder that Japan is still quite young in geological terms. The last big one, the Great Kanto Earthquake of 1923, killed 142,000 people and, since records show that a big earthquake comes every 60 years, Tokyo is long overdue for the next one. More recently, in January 1995, the Great Hanshin Earthquake in Kobe killed more than 5000 people and left many thousands homeless. Most cities have a citizen's handbook available in English which details what to do in an earthquake. There's also Disaster Prevention Day every September on the anniversary of the Great Kanto Earthquake, when emergency drills and prevention procedures are reviewed throughout the country.

What to do if you're in an earthquake

- If you're inside, dive under a table or other solid structure like a doorway.

- Turn off gas appliances such as stoves (most damage from earthquakes is caused by fires after the tremor).

- Open a nearby door or window to prevent it jamming, thus providing an escape hatch when the quake has stopped. Some people in high risk areas even have their furniture bolted to the walls and floor for added safety.
- If you're outside get to a clearing, such as a park, and avoid narrow streets and high walls.

Where there are earthquakes, there are *tsunami*, but they rarely cause the devastation that earthquakes cause. Iwate prefecture in northern Honshu is often hit by massive *tsunami*, triggered by offshore earthquakes. You'll often hear *tsunami* warnings, particularly if you live in a coastal area: I can remember three occasions when I was surfing and my friends and I were ordered out of the water by policemen with megaphones warning of an approaching tidal wave (on all three occasions we found out later that the '*tsunami*' measured only 30 cm or so, but better safe than sorry). We were also advised that if there was ever an earthquake in our city we should jump in the car and literally 'head for the hills' (higher ground) in case a *tsunami* followed. Sometimes an earthquake as far away as the other side of the Pacific (say, Chile) will cause a *tsunami* alarm in Japan.

Typhoons (aka tropical cyclones or hurricanes) are a more regular and generally less scary occurrence. Typhoon season is from July to October when about 20 typhoons are generated in the tropical mixing-pot around the equator before swirling their way north to Japan. They often head over to Taiwan and China, but if they continue north and bump into Japan they can cause anything from heavy rain and gale force winds to huge seas, landslides, flooding and destruction of houses and crops.

At the other extreme, Japan occasionally has droughts. The last major one occurred in 1994 when the rice crop was severely affected and Japan had to import foreign rice. Soaring temperatures in summer often lead to water shortages and rationing in some prefectures.

In addition to all this, Japan is the third most densely populated country on earth (imagine New Zealand with 120 million or the UK with twice as many people and you get the idea) and because most of the country is so mountainous, 75% of its population is squeezed onto the now overcrowded river plains. The result is 127 million people living on the habitable fringe of a highly unstable landscape. It's no wonder the Japanese tend to have a philosophical attitude towards life and a healthy respect for the elements.

A brief history of Japan

Knowing something about past events helps us understand why things happen as they do today. This very brief outline of Japan's history shows how key events, people and ideas have shaped the country and its beliefs and culture.

According to Japanese mythology, the islands of Japan were conceived from the union between the god Izanagi and his sister Izanami. Later, Izanami gave birth to the sun in the form of the Sun Goddess, Amaterasu. The grandson of Amaterasu was the first god to set foot on earth (in Miyazaki, actually) and in doing so, gave rise to the Japanese Imperial Line and the entire human race as we know it.

It's not as far-fetched as it sounds: there was a time when it was widely believed that all life came from the sun. So Japan, being the easternmost land in the known world and where the sun rose first (still symbolised by the rising sun on the national flag) seemed a logical place for life on earth to begin. (The idea that the emperor at least was descended from the Sun Goddess was used to strengthen allegiance to Japan during the Second World War before it was officially denounced by Emperor Hirohito in 1946.)

Mythology aside, it's believed that the first humans to set foot on Japanese soil were Caucasians who crossed a land bridge from eastern Siberia around 100,000 years ago. The Ainu (Japan's indigenous people) are the descendants of these migrants; they were pushed north by subsequent migrations (from China and Korea) and today around 14,000 Ainu live on reservations in Hokkaido. Hokkaido was not formally made part of Japan until 1868.

When the seas rose at the end of the Ice Age about 12,000 years ago, Japan was cut off from the mainland. As a result, although many aspects of Japanese culture came from China (*kanji*, chopsticks and Zen Buddhism) and Korea (the *kimono*), Japan evolved quite independently of these countries. Today's Japanese often feel more kinship with Western cultures than with Asian cultures; more Japanese people holiday in Hawaii, Australia, London, Paris and Rome than in Asian capitals; and the Japanese tend to feel unique relative to other Asians, that's if they consider themselves Asians at all. They're just Japanese.

The first Japanese, having arrived from China and Korea, stayed on the coastal fringe. They were fishermen (the Japanese love of fishing and fish persists) as well as nomads and hunter–gatherers. But in 300 BC all that changed. Wet rice cultivation was introduced into Kyushu from the nearby Korean peninsula, changing the lives of the Japanese forever. No more roaming! Communities had to settle and the people became reliant on the seasons (festivals are still held to celebrate phases of the moon, thank the gods for a good harvest and bless newly planted crops) and more team-oriented (the importance of the group and group harmony over the needs of individuals is still emphasised today).

'The family that farms together stays together' must have been the motto of the time, as communities clustered together to share resources and compete with outside communities, not unlike Scotland's Highland clans. The most powerful—which was actually the result of a merger of several strong communities—was the Yamato clan, which later established control over the whole country.

When Chinese writing arrived, it allowed the Yamato nobles to read many Chinese classics, including those by Confucius, and Buddhist texts. Buddhism gradually became very powerful and in Nara (where the Yamato head of state resided) many Buddhist temples and images of Buddha were constructed, making Nara an important stop on the tourist trail today.

By 800 AD, however, Buddhism was starting to get out of hand. The emperor, fearing that it was becoming more powerful than he was, ordered the capital to be moved to a new site, Kyoto, far away from the Buddhist stronghold of Nara. Now free of that 'bad old' Chinese and Korean influence, the Japanese really started developing a culture for themselves based on their own needs and talents. Shinto, Japan's national religion, grew in importance (today it's common for people to practise both Buddhism and Shintoism), Japanese systems of writing were developed (*hiragana* and *katakana* are still used in conjunction with *kanji*), art forms such as *ikebana* and calligraphy were refined and Japanese literature flourished. It was about this time that the world's first novel, *Tale of the Genji*, was written by Murasaki Shikibu, a woman courtesan in the 11th century.

Now the problem was that the ruling, reading and artistic elite were so engrossed in their creative pursuits that they were neglecting the everyday governing of their kingdoms. With their heads firmly in their books they failed to notice the rise and rise of the new kids on the block, the *samurai* or warrior class.

The first *samurai* were honourable bodyguards whose duty was to protect and serve their feudal lord. They prided themselves on endurance, self-control and showing no emotion (qualities still valued in Japanese society today) and, to avoid a dishonourable surrender in battle, developed the technique of ritual suicide known as *harakiri*. This involved the warrior kneeling to the ground and plunging his own sword into his body, while his aide supervised and, at the appropriate moment, lopping off his head. (During the Second World War, the belief that surrender was a disgrace, was reflected in the way the Japanese treated their prisoners of war.)

The *samurai* muscled their way into government. The emperor was kept as a mere figurehead with few powers while the military, headed by the supreme military commander, the *shogun*, set about running the country.

Around this time, the Mongols, led by Kublai Khan, tried to get into the act. They'd already entered Korea and in 1274 and 1281 staged invasions of Japan. Both were foiled, the latter one most dramatically when the Mongol fleet comprising 100,000 troops hit a freak typhoon off the coast of Kyushu. The relieved Japanese nicknamed this typhoon *kamikaze* ('divine wind'), believing that the gods had sent it to protect them from the nasty Mongols. (During the Second World War, the Japanese tried to repeat their good fortune of the past by calling their suicide pilots sent on one-way bombing missions, *kamikaze* pilots.)

After this major victory (or at least successful defence of the coastline) the *shogun* fell out of favour, largely because he couldn't afford to pay his soldiers. And following a period of sustained civil war, the emperor was restored.

A few emperors later, Japan had its first contact with non-Asian *gaijin* in the form of Portuguese traders shipwrecked off the coast of southern Kyushu. They were heartily welcomed, largely because of their great skill in producing weaponry. A few years later (it's now 1549) Jesuit missionaries arrived in the same region and proceeded to convert to Christianity a few of the local lords who had their sights set on foreign trade and foreign arms.

It seemed like a good idea at first. Converts to Christianity reached the thousands, particularly around Nagasaki, a city now known for its European flavour (Nagasaki is perhaps more multicultural than many cities of comparable size and has many historic sites dating back to this time). But that soon changed with the new emperor, Hideyoshi. He saw Christianity as a threat to his rule and set about making it illegal. To make sure no-one missed the point, in 1597 he ordered the crucifixion of 26 foreign priests and Japanese Christians. (Despite this setback, Christianity continued to thrive underground until it came up for air 300 years later with another period of foreign contact).

There followed an almost paranoid fear of things foreign. For the next 200 years, Japan had virtually no contact with the outside world. The Dutch, Chinese and Koreans already in the country were allowed to stay but only under strict supervision. (Today there's still a system of alien registration for all foreigners, which even includes Japanese-born Koreans). The Japanese were forbidden to travel abroad, an action punishable by death. (Until as late as the mid-1960s most Japanese nationals couldn't obtain passports, and so were unable to travel overseas. And while the new generation of travellers seems to be making up for lost time with ever-increasing numbers of tourists traversing the globe, overseas travel is still a relatively new concept.) Japan was a hermit, focused on developing its own culture and keeping the peace, while Western Europe embarked on the Industrial Revolution.

This state of affairs may have continued indefinitely if not for one thing: the rest of the world wanted Japan to come out and play.

Edo (now Tokyo), was fast becoming a huge city and many countries, including Russia, England and France, wanted a piece of the action. In 1787 Edo was the largest city in the world with 1.4 million people (Tokyo's population is now around 12 million). The turning point came in 1853 when the US, represented by Commodore Perry, boldly sailed into Tokyo Bay and threatened to blow the Imperial Palace to smithereens if he was not permitted to meet with the emperor. Needless to say, his request was granted and Japan was opened like an oyster to the world.

This submission had consequences for the emperor. Anti-government feelings were running so high that the *shogun* resigned as leader of the nation, leaving Japan without a strong, central government. It was during the subsequent Meiji Restoration (1853–1868) and the Meiji Era (1868–1912) that Japan began to catch up with the industrial world. Having oscillated between the rejection of everything foreign, fervent nationalism and acceptance of the new foreign ways, Japan settled into a balanced approach to the world, assessing what was 'out there' in terms of what could be of value to Japan.

Japan joined the world with all guns blazing, literally, by defeating China (1894–5) and Russia (1904–5) and annexing Taiwan (then called Formosa) and Korea. At the conclusion of the First World War, Japan was recognised as one of the Big Five nations of the world and to prove it, launched a full-scale invasion of China in 1937 after seizing Manchuria in 1931 and setting up a puppet government there.

By 1940, Japan had visions of a brave new Asian world (under Japanese rule) and saw the US as its main obstacle. Much controversy still clouds the events leading up to Japan's entry into the Second World War, but the widely-accepted view is as follows. After failing to persuade the US to promise neutrality, Japan launched a surprise attack on Pearl Harbour in Hawaii on 7 December 1941 which drew the US into war against Japan. There followed numerous battles in Asia, the Pacific and around Australia's northern shores. (Darwin lived in constant fear of being bombed by Tojo, the nickname for the Japanese; Aussie band The Hoodoo Gurus even wrote a song about it.)

Three years later, things were looking grim for the Japanese forces. Its cities had suffered heavy aerial bombing (this is one reason Tokyo is the gleaming new city it is today) and its military was under increasingly stiff attack. But the events that broke Japan's spirit were the atomic bombs dropped on Hiroshima on 6 August 1945 and, three days later, on Nagasaki. Citizens in both cities still have memorial services every year to remember the victims. In Hiroshima almost 200,000 people died and many still suffer from the radiation effects of the bombings. Japan was forced to surrender unconditionally. To add insult to injury, the then Soviet Union seized four small islands to the north of Hokkaido after the war. These Northern Territories, as they're known in Japan, are still a controversial topic in diplomatic circles and no peace treaty has been signed despite the fact that in 1956 both parties agreed to do so.

At the end of the war, Japan was reduced to a whimpering pile of rubble. Two million Japanese had been killed and with only 10% of the industrial capacity it had at the beginning of the war, its economy was in tatters. It was occupied by Allied forces commanded by General Macarthur and, although the occupation ended in 1952, the southern island of Okinawa was only returned to Japan in 1972. (As of October 1999, more than 50,000 American military personnel and civilians live in a 'little America' compound on Okinawa with American schools, shops and restaurants, although moves are afoot to close the base due to local feeling.) An American-approved constitution took away the emperor's political power and rendered the military impotent. (The Japanese military became the Japan Self Defence Force which, until 1995, was not permitted to enter conflicts beyond its own shores. Now it is allowed to serve with UN peacekeeping operations overseas.) The flip side of reducing Japan's defence spending to 1% of the national budget was that it allowed Japan to focus on developing its economy.

Japan's phenomenal economic growth since the war has spawned a number of theories and accompanying stereotypes to explain it, the most typical being those that portray the Japanese as a race of highly efficient, 'company-at-all-costs' workers. The social changes that have occurred alongside this economic growth have received less attention but are no less miraculous: Japan has managed to keep crime, unemployment, homelessness and other social evils at low levels that most other countries can only dream about. Having been focused on recovery for the last 50-odd years, Japan is now in its own 'golden age' and despite ongoing economic problems is still a dominant force in electronics, robotics, computer technology and car production which has led to an enormous trade surplus. Maybe the future will see Japan becoming more environmentally friendly and more worldly.

Culture shock

It's natural to feel some culture shock when diving into a new culture, and Japan can seem very odd at times, not just to the first-timer. It's a place of contradictions and surprises at every turn. Grown women, even mothers, wear their hair in pigtails like schoolgirls. The air is so polluted there are oxygen bars where you can hook up to a cylinder of O_2. People have 'sensorised' stuffed animals as pets. Blowing your nose is taboo, but it's quite OK to urinate in public. There are coffee shops with names like 'Heart and Coffee Groovy' and products such as Dole milk and an isotonic drink called Calpis. As for car names, where else in the non-English speaking world would you find a Suzuki We've?

There are two ways to cope with culture shock. One is to familiarise yourself with the culture before you go (which is the aim of this chapter). The other is, once you get there, to go easy on yourself—don't expect to adjust to Japan straight away. It takes time. Also, be careful not to judge things on your first impressions; things aren't always as they seem. Keep your mind as well as your eyes open. As soon as you think you've figured something out, you'll see something to completely contradict everything you've witnessed up to that point. But think of it this way, at least Japan is never boring. There's always something to amuse or confuse you. You'll notice something you don't like (such as the pollution) and then find a contrasting place or situation (like a clean sandy beach—they do exist!). You'll meet some people who'll always treat you as an outsider and others who will become your friends for life. That's Japan.

On being a *gaijin*

One of the first things you'll notice is that everyone is Japanese, there's not the mix of cultures we have in our home countries. Only about 1% of Japan's population is non-Japanese, and they're mostly Korean, Filipino or Chinese. This means that Western-looking people are still something of a novelty, particularly outside the main cities. In immigration-speak, we're known as 'aliens'. But to the average Hiroshi in the street, you and I are *gaijin* (outside person) or more politely—although there's some controversy over the best term—*gaikokujin* (foreign country person).

Being blonde and tall, that was pretty weird, because I felt like I was constantly on display, which irritated me if I had a cold or something and really wanted to blend in. So that took a bit of getting used to. Wendi Aylward

So, you're an outsider. As a newcomer it won't be so surprising because you'll *feel* like an outsider, but even foreigners who've lived in Japan for years still encounter these feelings of separateness. That's why it's a good idea to be prepared for the following experiences:

People staring at you, especially kids. You'll attract major stares if you do bizarre *gaijin* things like blow your nose or kiss someone in public. Unless you like this kind of attention, it's a good idea to try and understand what an unusual sight you are and adhere to local customs as much as you can.

People not understanding your Japanese, or not even being aware that you're speaking their language. For many Japanese, particularly those in country areas, it's a shock to see their language coming out of a foreigner's mouth and they can't reconcile what they're hearing with what they're seeing. The best response is patience and perseverance.

Being called an *America-jin* (America-person). There's a widespread belief that every foreigner in Japan is American with the result that whenever kids see a foreigner they call out "Hey, American!". If you are, that's fine, but if you're not, the best response is to ignore them, or if they're still within earshot you can call back, '*Chigaimasu. Australia-jin/New Zealand-jin/Canada-jin/Iglis-jin desu*' ('No, I'm Australian/New Zealander/Canadian/English').

Some people's ignorance about things in the outside world, even basic things like where your country is (particularly if you're from New Zealand) or that the seasons are reversed in the Southern Hemisphere. You can deal with this by telling people about your home town and what the weather's like there now, or about your family, and show them photos of your country.

Feeling like the 'token foreigner' or 'pet foreigner' on some occasions. In some places in Japan being with a *gaijin* is still something of a status symbol. It's usually harmless (they'll just want their friends to see you hanging out with them), and often has fringe benefits like being shouted to dinner. The best response is to go along with it until you learn to distinguish this kind of attention from genuine interest in you as a person.

Some Japanese are very interested in learning English and they'll ride you for that English. Other Japanese are more interested in you; those are the people you should make friends with. Vince Panero

Being complimented out of all proportion to your actual ability, particularly for your skill at wielding chopsticks or your grasp of the Japanese language. It's usually a sincere attempt to make you feel comfortable, though it may have exactly the opposite effect. Best just to act modest and deny any expertise by shaking your head or saying '*Mada mada*' ('I've got a long way to go yet').

Racial discrimination. Despite the homogeneity of its population, Japan isn't free of racial discrimination. In fact with so few non-Japanese, it makes it even harder for minority groups to gain acceptance. Discrimination towards *gaijin* comes in various forms: from being refused accommodation because the owners don't want the anticipated hassle of dealing with a foreigner, to being refused work because you may not look like a 'typical' (i.e. Anglo Saxon) foreigner.

Coping with the culture

When you think about any Japanese custom there are really only two things to remember. First, RELAX. As a foreigner you're not expected to know the ins and outs of Japanese culture, you're

© *The Alien* (1996) Reprinted with permission.

expected to make mistakes and you're always graciously forgiven if you do. The second thing to remember is RESPECT. This is the essence of all things Japanese and if you don't know the specifics but can remember to respect your hosts, your boss, your elders, and, in fact, everyone you meet, you can't go wrong.

Taking off shoes and sitting on the floor must be the quintessential Japanese customs. In fact, they go together. You can't sit, sleep and live on the floor if it's not clean and the best way to make sure it stays clean is to take off your shoes before you enter a room. Not only that but taking off your shoes is relaxing, puts everyone on an equal footing (so to speak) and makes things less formal.

It's usually clear when and where to take off your shoes. When you enter a house, apartment or hotel, the entrance will be at street level and you'll leave your shoes here before stepping up into the main part of the building. Don't be surprised if your shoes are pointing towards the street ready for you to step into when you leave; it's good manners on the part of your host to do this. There may be different sets of slippers for the kitchen/hallway and the bathroom. Remember to leave the slippers in the room where you found them, wearing the toilet slippers all over the house is a definite no-no! You should only wear socks or bare feet in the *tatami* (straw-matted) rooms. In most offices and shops, and an increasing number of Western-style homes, you can keep your shoes on.

Sitting on the floor gets more comfortable the more you do it. Don't worry if at first your knees seize up from folding your legs under or around you. It's quite OK to change positions as often as you need to, just don't point your outstretched legs at anyone or at an altar (it's bad form). You're usually sitting on flat cushions arranged around a low table, and in winter a heater is attached to the underside of the table with a quilt over the top. There are even electric carpets to sit on, a distant cousin of the electric blanket, same principle only it's designed to beat those draughty floors in winter.

Bathing is the next most important thing to know about Japanese culture. Whether it's at an inn or someone's house, or even an outdoor hot spring pool, the procedure's the same and it's one which must be followed carefully.

- Get undressed in the change room. Put your clothes in a locker or one of the baskets provided. Leave your towel in the change room (it'll get soggy if you take it into the steamy bath area). Most people just take a small towel, a bit like a large washer (it's often BYO, though you might be given one to use at some establishments), which they use to scrub themselves with when washing, and to hold in front of certain body parts when walking around the bath area.

- Enter the bath area. These vary enormously in size and style: from a single tub to those that resemble the Lost City of Atlantis with multiple pools, each filled with water of different temperatures or containing different therapeutic minerals, a few fountains and statues of small boys. In most homes the bath is a square tub, about one square metre and about thigh deep, which you crouch in with your knees up to your chest (not that you have much choice).

- Wash yourself *before* getting into the bath. This is the crux of the whole operation. In Japan a bath is for soaking, not washing. In fact the Japanese tend not to think too highly (to put it mildly) of the European custom of soaking in your own dirty bath water; not that anyone will say anything to you if you do it wrongly but there'll be a lot of covert embarrassment. You'll see a row of shower heads, usually at waist height. The idea is to sit on a low stool at one of the showers, wash yourself with soap (often provided), shampoo your hair if you like, and rinse off all the soap and shampoo by filling a plastic basin from the shower and pouring water over yourself.

- Finally you can get into the bath. Soak for as long as you like: most people spend at least an hour at the bathhouse or hot spring pool. Usually you wash again after getting out, particularly at the hot springs where there are a lot of mineral salts in the water. If you're in someone's home, it's usual for several family members (and guests) to use the same bath water, so don't pull the plug after you've finished.

Toilets are of two kinds, Western and Japanese. Japanese-style toilets are the same as those found throughout Asia and are rather unattractively called 'squat toilets', though that's exactly how you use them. They consist of an elongated ceramic bowl set into the floor. There's no seat, in fact you don't have to come in contact with the porcelain at all. You just squat, facing the hood with your feet placed either side of the bowl. You'll probably come across some unusual toilets in your travels through Japan: from those with computer controlled seat-warmers and bidet-style flushers, to those with toilet roll holders that play music. Since there's often no toilet paper in public toilets (nor any serviettes in most restaurants) it's a good idea to carry a pack of tissues in your bag; you'll soon get together a stash of these, as they're given out at train stations and service stations as promotional gifts.

Bedding also requires a different attitude. The Japanese sleep on *futons* laid directly on the floor. There's no bed base, but the floor's usually covered with *tatami* mats so it's got some spring in it. The *futons* are thinner than those generally available at home and are usually laid out each night just before going to bed, rolled up in the morning and stored in a cupboard during the day. This makes sense: having a 'fold-away' bed makes even the tiniest apartment look and feel quite spacious!

Japanese names are spoken and written with the family name first. Use *san* after someone's family name or their first name. You can also use one of the following variations: there's *chan* (for boys and girls) and *kun* (only for boys), but either can be used for adults when addressing close friends. For instance, my formal name is Louise-*san* but my Japanese friends call me Lou-*chan*. *Sama* is a special term reserved for highly respected individuals, such as sumo champions and school principals, but you often hear department store announcements addressing customers as *o-kyaku sama* (honourable customer). Never add *san*, *chan* or *kun* to your own name. If you're referring to yourself, use one of the forms of 'I': *watashi* (males and females), *atashi* (females only), or *ore* and *boku* (both for males only).

The Emperor. It's considered impolite to say the current emperor's name (Akihito) out loud in casual conversation. However, as the period of each emperor's rule is given a name, it's important to know at least two to understand how the Japanese write dates. These two are: Showa (1926–1989), because your birth date falls in this one; and the current one, Heisei (it means 'Peace Generation'), which started in 1989 (so 2001 is the 13th year of Heisei). Dates on official documents as well as Use By dates for food are often written like this: Heisei year, month, day, e.g. 1 March 2001 will be written '13.3.1'. Japan also uses the American way of writing dates: month, day, year (as opposed to day, month, year in Australia, New Zealand or the UK) so this same date could also be written '3.1.01'.

Gift giving. In Japan it really is 'the thought that counts' since what you give is less important than your intention to give something: the aim of giving gifts being usually to maintain and promote harmony in relationships. The main occasions for gift giving are when visiting someone's home or returning from holidays (which explains the Japanese penchant for souvenir shopping when overseas; they're busy buying *o-miyage* or presents for all their friends and relatives stuck at home). You'll also score major points if, when moving into a new abode, you give a present to each of your new neighbours; it doesn't have to be anything big, something small from your home country would be fine. Food is a common gift, ranging from cakes and pastries to gift-boxed beer or gift-wrapped rockmelon, but on Valentine's Day there's a twist: it's the women who give chocolates to the men.

Safety is a big plus when living in Japan as it's one of the safest countries in the world. This, for me, was one of the joys of being in Japan. For the first time in my life I felt free to go anywhere I wanted at any time of the day or night, alone. Not only that, but people don't try to rip you off, public telephones are rarely vandalised and taxi drivers don't try to take you the long way home. You can even leave a bag or wallet in a public place like an airport departure lounge and if it hasn't been handed in to the nearest police box by a thoughtful citizen you can be confident it'll still be where you left it, hours later, contents intact. You can carry large amounts of cash on your person quite happily. In country areas you often don't need to lock your house or car: our postman used to leave mail on the front door mat (inside the front door) for us! (Remember, however, that most kinds of travel insurance won't cover you for things stolen from an unlocked car or house.) That said, entertainment districts of large cities anywhere in the world are notoriously dodgy and those in Japan are no exception, so treat them with caution. And beware the relaxed security consciousness when you return home. Time spent in Japan can lull you into a false sense of security.

You lose your paranoia about your possessions [in Japan]. You don't worry about anything, even your car or your house. I haven't even got a key for my house, it doesn't even lock! I've never had a key, I've never locked it. It's so safe. Every now and then some things get nicked, but that's the same everywhere, no matter how safe it is there's always someone ready to take advantage. You've really got to change your attitude when you go back home; you've got to start locking the car, the house, and carry less cash around with you. I went to this bar the other night [in Miyazaki, southern Kyushu] and I had about $200 in my wallet and I left my wallet on the counter. When I went back it was gone but someone was looking for me, holding it up, going 'Who owns this?' My wallet did get stolen in Osaka once, at a games centre, but a policeman told me games centres are the most dangerous places in Japan. Sean Carey, a New Zealander who used to teach English at a swimming school (the kids practise their English conversation between swimming lessons).

Tipping is not the done thing in Japan, although at some places (restaurants, taxis and service stations) a service fee is included in the price. No-one expects tips and some people may even feel offended if you offer them money for what they see as a friendly gesture, like helping you with your bags or giving you directions. The only time people give cash to each other is at weddings and funerals and then the money is handed over in a special envelope, since that's the polite way to handle cash.

Modesty rules in everything: the way you speak, behave and dress. Once you start living in a confined space, say one or two rooms, you'll start to appreciate and understand the Japanese ways. Like the need to be tidy, to put your *futon* away every morning and consider your neighbours. It's probably safe to say that if you put 127 million Westerners in a country the size of Japan, it wouldn't be anything like the success story Japan has been.

I think the Japanese, especially in Tokyo, have an amazing ability to live together. This is obvious if you look at statistics, like criminal statistics, how low the crime rate is here. But if you just look at people together, I mean the kind of situations I ran into in Tokyo would drive the average American or Australian bonkers, like being crammed into a train. But they all just seem to go along with it. I guess you could be negative about it and say they're all just a bunch of robots, but they're people just like anybody else. It takes a lot of mental fortitude to distance yourself far enough away from that, to be peaceful in yourself to stand there and be in such close quarters. Peter Moses

A few comments to help you adjust to living at close quarters with others:

- Opinions are often withheld, and people tend to be make observations rather than positive or negative judgments about things.

- *Hai* (yes) rarely means 'yes' in the way we use it, since speaking directly is thought to be somewhat arrogant at best, and downright rude at worst. So what does *hai* mean? It can roughly be translated as 'what you've said is right', 'I understand what you've just said' or 'I hear you'; but it can also mean various shades of 'maybe', 'I don't understand', 'I don't know', 'I'll have to think about it', 'I'll check with my superior' or 'yes'!

- People are reluctant to contact people they don't know. Who you know and word-of-mouth recommendations are the two main lubricants in Japanese society. Meet as many people as you can, make friends and nurture all your relationships, whether socially or at work, and you'll have Japan at your feet. When trying to get things happening (e.g. when looking for an apartment), using ads or fliers is going about it the hard way. Instead, try asking for advice and talking to people (including other *gaijin*) and you'll often have more success.

- A smile is worth a thousand words. Japanese people smile when they're happy or amused, but they can also smile when they're nervous or embarrassed, or when they're not sure what to do next. So don't think the staff at your local bank are pleased to see you frustrated or struggling with your application for a new account, they're probably as uncomfortable with the situation as you are.

- Whilst people tend to avoid confrontations and direct expression of feelings, don't make the mistake of thinking the Japanese have no feelings. Public displays of emotion are just frowned upon. Showing anger or impatience closes the door: try to keep your cool in annoying situations and you'll be able to stay in the game. Group harmony, and managing not to offend anyone, is generally regarded as more important than individual expression. If you want to raise a specific issue, do it subtly or mention it discreetly at a social gathering: 'A word in your ear, my lord'.

Body language is important in most countries but crucial in Japan. Non-verbal communication includes subtle movements and changes in body position or tone of voice, and many others, all of which give subtle clues about what's really going on.

You have to really listen to them and not just with your ears but physically. Watch what they're doing with their body; if they're kind of fidgeting that means they're uncomfortable, or you've put them in a strange situation and they don't really know how to deal with it. You just have to really tune in to them ... you have to operate on a deeper level compared to Western culture where we just say something and it's out there. Alda Borror, an American working as an English teacher.

Body language doesn't always translate well. It's often easier to misunderstand body language than the spoken word; when learning a new language we expect to misunderstand speech, yet take the interpretation of body language for granted.

- It took me months to get used to the hand gesture for 'Come here' (a raised arm with the hand moving towards the gesturer) since it looks incredibly like 'Go away!'

- Any form of physical contact, except with really close friends or family (and sometimes not even then) is likely to get an embarrassed response. It's not even the done thing for married couples to show affection in public and it wasn't so long ago that it was customary for a wife to walk one step behind her husband whenever they were out together. But this is changing. Touching is becoming more common, sometimes you see young couples holding hands while walking down the street and many Japanese express a desire for the closeness between family and friends they see in American movies and TV shows. Still, be prepared: being hugged by a big friendly *gaijin* can be a little overwhelming for some Japanese.

- Pointing with your finger can be offensive. In Japan, people use their whole hand to indicate a direction or something they want to show you 'over there'. If you want to indicate yourself, point at your nose.

- Waving your hand back and forth across your face or crossing your hands in front of your chest to make an 'X' means something is *dame* (no good or not allowed).

Let's talk about sex. You could write a book on the subject of romantic liaisons (to put it nicely) between Japanese and *gaijin*, and some people have. *Bachelor's Japan* by Boye de Mente includes chapters such as 'Necking in Japan', 'Cars as Bachelor Accessories', 'Fertility Festival Anyone?', 'Why Foreigners like Japanese Women' and 'Foreigners Are Sex Happy'. *Making Out in Japanese* by Todd and Erika Geers is a phrasebook dealing with dating, relationships and social situations including how to ask a Japanese person out on a date, and how to have a fight with your loved one in Japanese.

In 1999 Japan finally approved the Pill as a means of contraception (before then, doctors could only prescribe it as treatment for other medical conditions) but condoms are still the contraceptive of choice: you can pick them up almost anywhere, even vending machines (for those late night emergencies!). If you're using the Pill, it's best to take your own supply, take a copy of your prescription with you and make sure you know the generic name, not just the brand name.

Following are a couple of contrasting experiences from veterans of the relationship scene in Japan, who shall remain nameless.

I learned the intense difference between having a relationship with a Westerner and having a relationship with a Japanese woman. Totally different jungle. Something that you can only really understand by experiencing it, but a few tips: Use condoms (of course). Go for it, but be incredibly sensitive. Realise that your average Japanese woman will fall in love three times as fast and ten times as deep as your average Western woman. Why this is, is because it's such a sensitive culture. If you don't realise this you can really hurt somebody that you'd never thought you'd hurt, just by small things. It's complicated, it's a labyrinth, but it's cool. Japanese women are very attractive, they're exotic. There's a willingness with Japanese women, a willingness to get into a relationship and get deep quickly, so if you're interested in getting into a deep relationship quickly it can happen here. Anonymous

Japanese girls tend to be very clingy and very jealous. There are certain rules set up that you may not be aware of at the outset: like you're not allowed to have any female friends outside your relationship. They tend to be very marriage-oriented, which can be good or bad depending on your point of view. And Japanese women tend to be very demure, to the point of being annoying! But they can be very lovely and beautiful too. It's not so common to see Western girls with Japanese guys because I think Western girls have been brought up in a different culture. Obviously it's a case-by-case thing and there are more and more, especially younger Japanese guys, who are very equality-minded and considerate. But on the whole Japanese men are dominant in the culture, just like in other Asian cultures. Male children are really coddled by their mothers, probably by their sisters, then by a girlfriend. I've met Japanese men who take pride in the fact that they've never washed their own clothes! So I think it's harder for Western women to get used to that. But it's the opposite for a foreign man and a Japanese woman, it's much more natural. It's not rethinking your whole culture, it's kind of a relaxed version of what you've been taught. Anonymous

Bowing replaces the handshake and a whole lot more in Japan. *Gaijin* aren't expected to bow, but just so you know: the lower your status the lower you bow, usually from the waist, with a straight back and your arms at your sides. In most situations, a small bow is enough, even a nod. Also use bowing when driving to signal 'thank you' or 'go ahead', instead of using a hand gesture.

Business cards (*meishi*) are essential. It's been said that you don't exist in Japan unless you have a *meishi*, which at its simplest is a card with just your name on it, which is very helpful for spelling those tricky *gaijin* names and proof that you are who you say you are. It doesn't have to be in Japanese, although that will help if you're trying to find private English students or find work in a Japanese company. But even if the Japanese can't understand your card, it's just good form to exchange cards, a gesture that says you've come to Japan prepared to try and fit in with some of the customs.

When you give someone your business card, hold it out in both hands with the writing facing them so they can read it straight away (as they will). When you receive someone else's card, the standard procedure is to take it with both hands and read it; even ask a question about some part of it, or say the company name or the person's name out loud to show you're reading it. Never write on someone else's card or put it in your back pocket (where it could be sat on).

If you have a cold, sniff, don't blow. Blowing your nose in front of other people is considered bad form. If you must blow your nose, use a tissue, not a handkerchief (Japanese regard these as disgusting) and do it discreetly. If you come to work while you're ill, don't be offended if your boss asks you to wear a surgical mask to avoid spreading germs. This is seen as a common courtesy to your fellow workers or students.

Japanese superstitions are pretty different to the ones most of us grew up with. The number four often carries connotations of bad luck since the *kanji* for 'four' is similar to the *kanji* for 'death'. That's why there often won't be apartment numbers or house numbers with a four, just as Western hotels, office blocks or hospitals don't have a 13th floor. It's also believed to be bad luck to cut your toenails at night, wear new shoes in the evening, sew a button on before you leave the house or see crows flying over your house. But just to balance it out, there are lots of good omens too: it's good luck to sleep with your head pointing north, see a shooting star or find a tea stalk standing on end at the bottom of your cup. And when a child loses a tooth, you're supposed to throw it (the tooth) over the roof of your house (too bad if you live in an apartment block) for good luck.

Chinese astrology is more commonly talked about than Western astrology in Japan. The Chinese zodiac contains 12 animals, with each animal representing a different year. People exchange cards at Chinese New Year (with cards depicting the animal for the coming year), usually sometime in February, the way we exchange Christmas cards. It's also common for people to display pictures or models of the animal for the current year in their homes and offices to bring them luck. The calendar New Year is also celebrated on 1 January (just to be sure!).

Most people know the Chinese animal for the year they were born. If you want to know your animal 'sign' check the following list of animals and recent years, and if you want to say, 'I was born in the year of the snake' say, '*Watashi wa hebi doshi desu.*'

Rat (*nezumi*) – 1972, 1984	Horse (*uma*) – 1966, 1978
Ox (*ushi*) – 1973, 1985	Sheep (*hitsuji*) or
	Goat (*yagi*)–1967, 1979
Tiger (*tora*) – 1974, 1986	Monkey (*saru*) – 1968, 1980
Rabbit (*usagi*) or Cat (*neko*) – 1975	Rooster (*tori*) – 1969, 1981
Dragon (*tatsu*) – 1964, 1976	Dog (*inu*) – 1970, 1982
Snake (*hebi*) – 1965, 1977	Pig (*inoshishi*) – 1971, 1983

Blood groups is another common topic of discussion for those newly acquainted. 'What's your blood group?' ranks right up there with 'How old are you?' and 'Are you married?' as questions *gaijin* are most often asked. The idea is that 'O' people (the majority) tend to be pretty normal and easy-going; 'B' people tend to be quite sociable and prefer working with people; 'A' people tend to be sensitive while 'AB' people are a mixture of A and B. Mind you, these definitions aren't set in stone and often even seem to vary the more people you ask!

Crossing the language barrier

You can learn a lot about a country and its culture by studying its language. In Japan this is particularly so because, unlike many other major languages, Japanese is not spoken in any other country.

Put simply, the Japanese language *is* Japan. For starters, there's the way the Japanese write their names—family name first, own name last—indicating the importance of the group over the individual. Similarly, when they refer to employees they put the company name first as in 'Sony's Mr Yamamoto' which shows the importance of being connected to a (often work-related) group. The words said before and after every meal indicate the importance of food and eating as a ritual in the Japanese culture. The fact that the word *iie* (no) is hardly used shows the Japanese reluctance to openly disagree, preferring instead to maintain group harmony.

The myth that Japanese is a difficult language. 'Most people can reach a surprising degree of fluency in colloquial Japanese in a relatively short time,' says Gary Brown, Registrar at the Australian Institute of Modern Languages (which incorporates the Japanese Language Institute in Sydney). Sure, the written system is tricky for us 'alphabetans' with over 2000 *kanji* plus two native Japanese 'alphabets'. But conversational Japanese isn't difficult, in fact Japanese has many aspects that make it easier than English or other Latin-based languages.

For instance, pronunciation is easy with only five vowels and 13 consonants. Consonants always occur with a single vowel (e.g. *ka*), never in multiples as in English (e.g. school). Each sound can only be said one way, unlike English where 'a' is pronounced differently in 'cat', 'father' and 'saw'. In Japanese 'a' is always pronounced 'ah' whether the word is '*arigato*', '*san*' or '*Osaka*'. So when you read a word you immediately know how to pronounce it even if you've never seen it before. Japanese speakers can pronounce all the sounds in the English language except 'l' and 'r' which don't occur in Japanese.

There are no articles (a, an, the) and words don't change when they become plural: *isu* (chair) is the same whether there's one chair or twenty. There's often no need for personal pronouns (he, she, him). So you can say something like '*mo tabemashita*' ('already eaten') and depending on who you're speaking to or your intonation, it can mean 'I've already eaten', 'he's already eaten', 'have you already eaten?' and so on.

The most difficult aspects of spoken Japanese are those concerning politeness and counting. Applying the correct level of politeness according to the person you're speaking to, and understanding different tones and words for men and women speakers is tricky, though this improves with practice. Although, being a *gaijin*, you're not expected to know these aspects straight away.

Counters are the words attached to things when you count them (in English, 'two' is the counter in 'two tables'). In Japanese this word changes with the thing that you're counting. Long, thin objects, for example, have different counters to flat objects. You can sneak around this problem by using the general words for numbers of things, e.g. *hitotsu* can refer to one piece of sushi, one dog, one car, or one of anything. (See 'Basic Phrases' in the Appendix for a list of counters.)

Do a Japanese language course before you go. If you don't already have some Japanese, doing a beginners' course before you go has several advantages:

- It'll give you an introduction to the culture, so you won't arrive in Japan completely 'green'. It can also be a chance to meet other people going to or coming from Japan, allowing you to swap information and stories.

- Australia and New Zealand are well set up for quality Japanese language courses, largely because Japan is a major trading partner for both countries, but most countries have a range of reputable Japanese language schools.

- Non-native Japanese speakers in your home country can often empathise better with your needs than teachers in Japan, and perhaps even give you advice on coping with Japanese culture.

- It will give you an idea of the best language learning materials available: tapes, dictionaries, phrasebooks and textbooks.

- When you get to Japan you'll probably want to save your hard-earned cash or spend it on more exciting things than a language course. Also, many courses in Japan require you to commit and pay in advance for several months of tuition. Besides, once you get there the whole country will be your classroom and everyone you meet, your teacher.

When choosing between schools or courses it's a good idea to check the following: class size (smaller is better); whether a compulsory text or class notes are included in the course fee; if a fee refund option is available if you're not satisfied; and the usefulness of the course for beginners.

Teach yourself *hiragana* and *katakana*. There are four ways to write Japanese: *kanji, romaji, hiragana* and *katakana*.

- *Kanji* are based on Chinese characters and although originally from China, many have been adapted to the Japanese spoken language. Each *kanji* is a picture that represents an idea, so it's very space-efficient and allows for intuitive comprehension. Nevertheless, *kanji* tend to be beyond the scope of most beginners learning Japanese.

- *Romaji* are English letters used to write Japanese words. You already know some *romaji*, e.g. *konnichiwa* (hello) is in *romaji*. Using almost all the letters we have in our alphabet, you can spell Japanese words so that non-Japanese speakers can read and pronounce them. *Romaji* is increasingly being used on product labels, in advertising and on signs, particularly at train stations, along main roads and in large hotels.

- *Hiragana*, are like simple *kanji* except that instead of representing a concept each one represents a sound such as *ta*, *so* or *mu* made up of a consonant and a vowel. It's handy to learn *hiragana* as it gives you an appreciation for Japanese pronunciation. The only problem is that even if you learn all 46 *hiragana* symbols, you can read very little since most written Japanese is composed of *kanji*, *hiragana* and *katakana*. Hence you end up only being able to read a few syllables. Sometimes you'll see tiny *hiragana*, called *furigana*, written above *kanji* so that Japanese people who can't read certain *kanji* (and foreigners) can understand the word.

- *Katakana* is like *hiragana*, except that *katakana* is used only for foreign (or foreign-derived) words. The 46 *katakana* characters are usually the first thing most *gaijin* learn because they help you read menus in places like McDonalds! *Katakana* often exist on their own, without *kanji* or *hiragana*, so you can at least read complete words and phrases. Still, even that can be a challenge when the English word and its Japanese derivative seem worlds apart. Try this quick quiz: What does *ma ku do na ru do* mean? (Hint: it's a fast food place with golden arches).

A checklist of things to do and take

- ☐ **Passport:** Make sure it's valid for however long your visa is valid.
- ☐ **Visa:** Check with your nearest embassy or consulate if you need a visa to visit Japan. Find out about requirements for working holiday visas and allow plenty of time to organise the application before you leave home.
- ☐ **Photocopies:** Leave a copy of your passport's front page, air ticket, visa and itinerary with your family or trusted friend. Take a second copy with you, stored separately to the originals.
- ☐ **Air ticket:** Remember to confirm your flight at least 72 hours before departure.
- ☐ **Book your first two or three nights accommodation in Japan:** A homestay can be a good option since it'll introduce you to a few of the locals while giving you a comfortable and affordable place to stay.
- ☐ **Gather information about Japan:** A good source of tourist and travel info is the Japan National Tourist Organisation which has 14 offices worldwide including Sydney, New York, Chicago, San Francisco, Los Angeles, Toronto and London (see Appendix for contact details). Most countries also have a Japan cultural centre as well, often within the Japanese consulate or embassy. The Japan Foundation has offices in Sydney, Toronto, New York, Los Angeles and London (see Appendix).

- □ **Travellers cheques:** Although Japan is one of the safest countries in the world, you might be taking a fair amount of money with you (e.g. the working holiday visa requires a minimum of US$2000 per person) so it's a good idea to take most of that in travellers cheques. Take some yen in cash with you as well.

- □ **International Driving Permit:** You'll need one of these to be able to drive a car or ride a scooter in Japan, at least until you've been living in Japan long enough to apply for a Japanese drivers licence. International permits are available from your national motoring association (e.g. RACV, NRMA, AA). In Australia the cost is about AUD$15. These permits are only valid in Japan for six months from the date of issue, after which you'll need to get a Japanese driving licence from the licence office (*shikenjo*). Bring your drivers licence from home, passport photos, Alien Card and the fee; you'll have to fill in a few forms and have an eyesight test.

- □ **Travel insurance or health insurance:** If you're staying less than six months and travelling around Japan, travel insurance is probably the best option, but if you're planning to work it's a good idea to look into companies that offer health insurance overseas (see Living chapter). No vaccinations are necessary for Japan but if you're thinking of travelling on to other countries, check the requirements. Make sure you check any insurance policy carefully—some won't cover you for work-related injuries or high risk activities such as skiing and abseiling.

- □ **Business cards:** It's handy to have a business card (even one with just your name) when you first arrive in Japan. Once you get settled, however, you can go for the 'deluxe' version— English on one side, Japanese on the other—which you can have printed for a minimal cost.

- □ **Your curriculum vitae/resume:** Take several copies, along with copies of any degrees, diplomas or certificates you have. Education is highly valued in Japan.

- **Passport-sized photos:** You'll need a few of these: two for alien registration; two to register at the Japan Association for Working Holiday Makers; and if you have to apply for jobs (particularly teaching jobs) by mail, your employer will generally want to see what you look like before deciding to interview you.

- **Prescription medications:** Talk to your doctor about whether additional prescriptions are necessary. This applies to the Pill as it can be difficult to obtain in Japan. Make sure you carry the actual prescription or a letter from your doctor with you when going through Japanese customs—Japan has ultra-strict regulations governing drug use. The prescription or letter should show the generic name and the brand name, since the same medication might exist in Japan under a different name.

- **Have checkups with your doctor and dentist:** Obtain any necessary treatment before you go since medical and dental costs in Japan rival those in the US for the title of 'world's most outrageous'.

- **Toiletries:** Take your preferred brands, at least enough to last until you've figured out what's what in the supermarkets. Things that can be hard to buy in Japan include good sunscreen, deodorant and mosquito repellent. Girls: BYO tampons, they're available but tend to be expensive. As for condoms, rumour has it that *gaijin* and Japanese sizes tend to be somewhat ... er ... different, so consider yourself warned and BYO. If you get desperate, there are condom vending machines in all the major cities.

- **Clothes:** Take shoes that are easy to slip on and off, since you'll be doing just that several times a day, every day; and comfortable clothes that make it easy to sit on the floor. Remember, you'll need the coolest clothes you can find for sweltering summers, and thermals, scarves and gloves, even overcoats, for winter. Definitely take a raincoat and when you get there, buy a cheap umbrella. You'll need both in the rainy season. To save lugging around a year's worth of clothes, pack up next season's gear before you leave and ask someone back home to mail it to you when you find a place to live (allow one to three months by sea mail). If you take a bigger than average size in shoes or clothes bear in mind that you might not be able to find your size in Japan.

- □ **Work clothes:** The word is 'conservative'. Appearance and image mean everything in Japan particularly in large cities and large companies. For women, this means a blouse, skirt (preferably above the knee, corporate-style), stockings (BYO, Japanese legs aren't the same size or shape as Western legs) and conservative shoes. For guys, business shirt and tie, trousers, shoes and socks, maybe a jacket for formal occasions. Long sleeved shirts are the norm, although there is a day in August when salarymen (company employees) all over the country are allowed to change over to their short sleeved shirts for the rest of summer. For jobs in smaller cities and small companies, you'll be allowed to dress more casually—shorts and sandals in summer and jeans in winter—particularly if you're only working part-time. Certain kinds of jobs, such as hostessing, have specific dress requirements.

- □ **Electrical appliances:** Japan operates on 100V electricity, a unique voltage that's hardly used anywhere else in the world. Most North American appliances will run quite happily in Japan as the power points (sockets) are the same while the voltage and hertz are close. With Japanese power points requiring plugs with two vertical pins to fit, Australians, New Zealanders and Europeans will need an adaptor for the plug and a transformer to boost the voltage up to the 220/240V required to run your appliances.

- □ **Power of attorney:** It's a good idea to give someone—usually a family member or close friend—power of attorney, so they can make bank deposits and withdrawals, and pay bills and credit card payments on your behalf. Ask at your bank before leaving home, it usually involves signing a simple form.

- □ **Make a will:** It might sound premature but it's a good idea to have a will, if only to ensure your wishes are carried out.

Look before leaping

- **Cancel any regular payments, organise direct debits or ask someone to pay bills for you while you're away:** This includes any subscriptions, regular bills and domestic health cover payments (you'll be covered by your travel insurance while in transit and when in Japan).

- **Take your name off the electoral roll:** Australians have compulsory voting and so this is a good idea if there's any chance of an election while you're away. Otherwise you'll have to go to an embassy or consulate of your home country (usually in Tokyo or Osaka) to vote.

- **Gift giving:** Stock up on small gifts. You never know when those miniature koalas or kiwis, pictures of the Queen or tiny Canadian flags might come in handy.

- **Information on your home country:** You'll be asked a lot of questions about your country and life back home. You'll probably know the answers to most of them but it helps to have a few props such as maps, photos, even gorgeous travel brochures. Remember, you're an unpaid diplomat!

- **Language books, dictionaries and phrasebooks:** These often cost less in Japan than back home, so it's worthwhile waiting until you get there to stock up.

- **Books and magazines:** You'll probably have a lot of free time when you first arrive so take those novels you've always wanted to read and a few of your favourite magazines, as they can be expensive in Japan (they also make great conversation starters in English classes!).

Arriving

When I flew to Osaka for the first time, I felt like I'd arrived in Japan before I'd even set foot on the plane. There I was in the JAL departure lounge in Sydney, the only blonde head as far as I could see (which was quite a long way considering I could see over everyone's heads). Before they even announced our flight was boarding, people started forming an orderly queue behind the gate. I was already a *gaijin*, in fact when we started boarding one of my fellow passengers (an elderly Japanese woman) even mistook me for a flight attendant! Then, as we taxied away from the terminal, I looked out my window to a vision I have never seen before or since: the entire Japan Airlines ground crew standing to attention and waving goodbye to the plane.

With at least nine hours flying time from Sydney to Japan (it's 13 from New Zealand, 9¾ from Vancouver, 13½ from Toronto, 11½ from LA, 13¾ from New York and 12 hours from London) you have time to adjust to the concept that you're soon to arrive in one of the world's most densely populated countries, not to mention one of its busiest international airports, usually Narita in Tokyo or Kansai in Osaka. But the concept is scarier than the reality.

The Japanese are experts at creating order out of chaos and this is evident in the vast, crowded spaces of its airports. Going through customs and immigration is a breeze: there may be thousands of passengers arriving and departing, but there are usually only a few foreigners on each flight so moving through the non-citizen immigration clearance desks takes no time at all. Plus, all of Japan's major airports have English-speaking staff and Tourist Information Centre (TIC) staff, as well as English signs and phones.

Changing money

You'll get a better exchange rate at a bank than at the airport, but you'll need some cash for your first few days. The question is:

How much? This really depends on where you're staying since accommodation will eat up the major portion of your expenses in the first few days. Don't be surprised or disillusioned if at first Japan seems as expensive as all those horror stories you've heard. It's easy to spend money in Japan's big cities, as in cities anywhere. Once you settle in, find a permanent place to stay, make a few friends and figure out how to do things cheaply, your living expenses will drop dramatically.

At first though you might have to bite the bullet and spend ¥6500-8500 per day: say ¥4000-5000 for hostel accommodation, ¥1000-2000 for three cheap meals and ¥1500 for transport and extras (figures supplied by the Japan National Tourist Organisation). More likely it'll reach ¥10,000 per day. It's a good idea to cash sufficient travellers cheques when you arrive to have about ¥40,000–50,000 in cash to save the hassle of going to the bank for at least the first few days. Don't worry about carrying this much cash on you, Japanese people do it all the time and it's generally quite safe. Credit cards are accepted in the main cities but not in smaller cities and rural areas.

The Tourist Information Centre (TIC)

There are TICs at Narita Airport and at Kansai Airport as well as in the major cities. Narita TIC is on the arrival floor of both Terminals 1 and 2 and is open from 9 am to 8 pm seven days a week. Kansai TIC is open 9 am to 9 pm seven days. Many TIC staff speak English. Tell them it's your first time in Japan and they'll be more than helpful. They'll probably load you up with an armful of brochures.

If you don't have any accommodation booked (it's a good idea to organise accommodation before you leave home), ask the TIC staff to help you find some for the first few nights. If you can afford it, staying in a Japanese-style place provides a great introduction to the culture. *Minshiku* are traditional family-run hotels where you sleep on futons in *tatami* rooms and use a traditional bath. However, many managers and staff in *minshiku* don't speak English. A *ryokan* is a more expensive, more traditional version of a *minshiku*. Other options include youth hostels, *gaijin* houses or guest houses, homestays, pensions and bed and breakfasts.

If there's no TIC at your arrival airport, you can use the Japan Travel-Phone service. Simply call the following numbers for English language travel advice and information from anywhere in Japan (you can't call these numbers from outside Japan):

- If you're not in Tokyo or Kyoto call 0088 224 800 toll free (9 am to 5 pm daily)
- In Tokyo call 03 3201 3331 (9 am to 5 pm every day except Saturday afternoons, Sundays and National Holidays, calls cost ¥10/minute)
- In Kyoto call 075 371 5649 (daily 9 am to 5 pm, calls cost ¥10/minute).

Getting out of the airport

The next step is getting to your accommodation. If you've organised a homestay for your first few nights, chances are you'll have someone to meet you. Otherwise you can ask at the TIC for an English language subway map and a few directions (which subway line, what's the nearest stop, etc). Never, ever take a taxi from an airport to the city, especially in Tokyo. A taxi from Narita to the city centre is liable to set you back up to ¥30,000 (around AUD$500). Most major airports have several options for getting to the city centre. If you have a Japan Rail Pass (purchased outside Japan), simply go to the JR station at the airport, validate your pass and hop on the Narita or Kansai Express train. (The Japan Rail Pass is not available to those with a working holiday visa.)

Following is an outline of the other main options.

In Tokyo

All international flights into Tokyo arrive at Narita Terminal 1 or 2. Unfortunately, Narita is 60 km east of Tokyo. To get to central Tokyo from Narita, choose one of the following options, all clearly signposted in English.

- The Airport Limousine Bus is the most popular option with one leaving every 10 to 15 minutes. It takes about 55 minutes to reach Tokyo City Air Terminal and from there it's a short taxi ride or subway trip to your final destination. The cost is ¥2900. If you go on to JR (Japan Rail) Tokyo station it takes 80 minutes and costs ¥3000. Buses also go to Shinjuku station, Haneda Airport and more than 60 major hotels. You can buy a ticket at the well-marked ticket office in front of the customs area. This is a good option if you have lots of luggage. Individual hotels such as Shiba Park also have their own shuttle buses.

- The Narita Express (NEX) train leaves from the station under the airport, takes 53 minutes to get to JR Tokyo station and costs ¥2940. The JR Airport Narita train takes 80 to 90 minutes and costs ¥1280. All the necessary signs and announcements are in English on this line. Call the JR East Infoline on (03) 3423 0111 Monday to Friday 10 am to 6 pm for information about JR East Trains, including NEX.

- Keisei Railways run the Skyliner train to Keisei Ueno station (a short walk from the main JR Ueno station which is the equivalent of Central Station in Tokyo). This takes 60 minutes and costs ¥1920. The Limited Express train takes 71 minutes and costs ¥1000.

To get to central Tokyo from Haneda (Tokyo's other, mainly domestic airport) you can do as the locals do and take the monorail to Hamamatsu-cho station (¥470) which takes 22 minutes. Otherwise take the Airport Limousine Bus (minimum charge ¥600) from Haneda to Tokyo station, Tokyo City Air Terminal, Narita Airport, hotels in the Akasaka, Shinjuku, Ikeburo, Makuhari, Maebashi-Takasaki and Chiba areas, and to Tokyo Disneyland and Tokyo Big Sight.

If you arrive at Narita and have to transfer to a domestic flight at Haneda, you can take the Airport Limousine Bus from Narita to Haneda. It leaves frequently and takes about 75 minutes and costs ¥3000.

In Osaka

Kansai Airport is the second largest airport and Japan's first 24 hour airport. When it was opened in September 1994 it was also the first airport in the world to be constructed on a man-made island (which is connected to the mainland by a bridge). It's in Osaka Bay about 60 km from central Osaka. Your options from Kansai Airport depend on where you want to go in Osaka and surrounding areas:

- To Osaka station, take the JR Rapid train which takes 65 minutes and costs ¥1160 or the Airport Limousine Bus which takes 65 minutes and costs ¥1300.

- For Shin-Osaka station, take the JR Limited Express train (Haruka) which takes 45 minutes and costs ¥2980, or a slower local train for ¥1320.

- For Tennoji station, take the JR Limited Express train (Haruka) which takes 29 minutes and costs ¥2270, or the slower local train for ¥1030.

- For Namba station, take the Nankai Railways Limited Express which takes 29 minutes and costs ¥1400, or a slower local train for ¥890.

- For Kyoto station, take the JR Limited Express train (Haruka) which takes 75 minutes and costs ¥3490, or a slower local train for ¥1830, or a bus which takes 1 hour 45 minutes and costs ¥2300.

- For Kobe City Air Terminal (KCAT), take the Kobe Jet Foil which takes 28 minutes for ¥2200 (price includes shuttle bus from airport to port).

- For Sannomiya station (Kobe), take a bus from KCAT which takes 15 to 20 minutes and costs ¥320. Alternatively take the JR Local train from Kansai which takes 84 minutes and costs ¥1660. The Airport Limousine Bus is a bit faster at 75 minutes for ¥1800. This bus also goes to Nara, Wakayama, Wakauraguchi and Amagasaki, Itami Airport, Kintetsu Railways Uehommachi station, Keihan Railways Moriguchi and Uji stations and the Hikone Prince Hotel at Lake Biwa.

From other airports

- From Itami Airport (Osaka's other airport), the Airport Limousine Bus goes to Kyoto station and major hotels in Kyoto, takes 60 to 100 minutes and costs ¥1280–1370. It also stops at a number of other railway stations.

- From Shin-Chitose Airport in Sapporo, take the JR Airport Express train to Sapporo station which takes about 35 to 40 minutes and costs ¥1040.

- From Nagoya Airport, take the Meitetsu Bus which goes to Nagoya station in 32 minutes and costs ¥870.

- From Fukuoka Airport, take the Fukuoka subway to Hakata station which is only about five minutes and costs ¥250.

First things first

Exploring

Getting used to a new country is like easing yourself into a hot Japanese bath. Don't be in a hurry to understand everything at first, you'll only end up scalding yourself. Give yourself a culture-break every now and then. Don't feel guilty if you crave a hamburger or a good cup of coffee, or find yourself sneaking into McDonalds. Every *gaijin* has done it and many keep doing it! Just go slowly, absorb everything and the pieces will fall into place by themselves if you let them.

Absorb all your first impressions. Remember, no-one else will notice all the things you notice, feel the same about what you see or have your memories. Of course you'll still have a lot in common with other foreigners who've walked the same streets. Whether you explore physically (on foot, by bicycle or on the subway) or mentally (by watching TV, listening to the radio, watching or eavesdropping on people in the street) it's important to get your bearings in a new place. I always like to know where I am in relation to the sea or the nearest river, or even just which way is west so I can watch a sunset.

A word on language exploration. You may already have had an introduction to the Japanese language. Now's the time to build on that preliminary knowledge. Even if you don't understand what you're hearing and even if it feels like a waste of time, you'll learn something every time you're exposed to a new language. It's like being a child again: you don't understand anything at first, but after a while the jumble of sounds starts to sort itself into recognisable blocks and you'll start to connect words to their meanings, even if you can't say the words yourself. Also, once you start getting out and about, you'll find out what you need to know, instead of what you were taught in a course, or what I might tell you here. Pick a situation you want to be able to deal with—like ordering a meal, buying a few stamps, catching a train or watching your favourite sport—and try to learn the vocabulary that goes with it, even just a few words.

Getting around on foot. Watch for bicycles on footpaths; sometimes the footpath will be divided into two lanes, clearly marked for bikes and pedestrians. Japanese drive on the LEFT, so if you're from continental Europe or North America, remember to LOOK RIGHT before crossing the road (everyone else should know by now!).

Travelling by bicycle. Most bikes are black, plain and gearless with a basket on the front. Mountain bikes don't seem to have caught on much except among *gaijin*. A good new bike can set you back up to ¥15,000 for your basic shopping model. A second-hand one might cost about ¥5000. Helmets aren't required by law, and most people don't bother. Everyone rides bikes—women in suits, businessmen on their way to work and high school kids (but not primary school kids as they're supposed to walk to and from school). Make sure you have a lock for your bike, and take note of a distinguishing feature of the bike or the lock when leaving it at a crowded bike-parking area like a train station. Some people even paint their names on the rear mudguard of their bikes. If you want to take your bike on the train, the wheels must be taken off and the whole thing wrapped up, either in a bag or some cloth or canvas. If you're in a city don't even think about putting a bike on a train during the busy times.

Using the trains and subways. Trains in Japan run like clockwork. Rarely late and always clean, they always seem to have the passengers' best interests at heart. Markings on the platform show where each carriage door opens when the train stops, allowing commuters to queue right in front of an open door. Most JR train and subway stations have signs showing the station name in English and *kanji*. Names of the last and the next station are also shown. Each line is represented by a different colour so you can learn the system by learning the colours.

The main rail company is Japan Railways (JR), a group of six companies that have tracks criss-crossing the entire country. JR is famous for its punctuality (in Tokyo peak hour trains run every 1½ minutes!) and JR stations are still central to each community or town. JR operates local and inter-prefecture trains as well as subways, buses, ferries and the *shinkansen* ('bullet train'). Other private railway lines usually operate short (less than 100 km) stretches of track.

The most economical way to travel around Japan is with a Japan Rail Pass, though there are a few catches: the Pass must be bought outside Japan, you can't buy one if you have a working holiday visa, and you can't travel on the new super express Nozomi train. The good news is that you get unlimited travel on JR lines and affiliated buses and ferries including the famed *shinkansen* ('bullet train') and a 10% discount at JR hotels, and the Pass allows you to see the country at much lower rates than you'd otherwise pay. There are 7, 14 and 21 day JR Passes available, starting at ¥28,300. If you plan to travel only in specific regions, you can buy a JR East Pass (for everywhere north of Tokyo), JR West Pass (for western Japan, west of Kansai International Airport) and JR Kyushu Pass (for all Kyushu). Contact your nearest Japan National Tourist Organisation for details.

Trains and subways don't run all night. So when you're out on the town, take note of when the last train on your line leaves (usually around midnight), otherwise you could be stranded until the next morning (the first trains start around 5 am) or be forced to party til dawn!

Women need to beware of crowded trains. There's a sub-species of male that likes to take advantage of the crowded conditions and the fact that you can't move easily, to feel the 'lie of the land' so to speak. If this happens to you, tell the culprit off loudly, even if you don't know who's doing it. Saying something like 'Stop It!', even in English, will usually work.

You buy train tickets for local services either at a machine or the station's ticket office. Smaller stations often have neither: just get on the train when it arrives and pay the conductor on board or the driver as you get off. To use a machine, do the following:

- Find your destination on the route map, usually above the ticket vending machines. For trains it'll usually be written in *romaji*, but for the subway it'll be in *kanji*, so try to recognise the *kanji* for your usual destinations. The figure below it will be the fare. This fare is for a single ticket—you can't buy return tickets from vending machines.

- Go to a machine, press the button corresponding to the fare you need (there'll be buttons for, say, ¥120, 150, 200 and 220 fares). The machines in major Tokyo subway stations have English instructions. The vending machines take ¥1000 notes, coins and prepaid cards like the JR Orange Card.

- Insert your ticket in the automatic gate as you go onto the station platform. Make sure you take your ticket as you pass through, as you'll need it at the other end.

If you're having trouble using the ticket machines, you've got two options. First, ask the person at the ticket window 'your destination *made wa ikura desu ka*' ('How much is it to my destination?') and buy the ticket there. Or, look on the route map for the lowest fare (usually ¥120 for subways, a bit more for the trains) and buy that. When you get to your destination, go to the fare adjustment window (*ryukin seisanjo*) before the exit gate. The collector will check your ticket and tell you how much extra (if any) you have to pay. Remember to keep your ticket with you after you get on the train or subway—you'll need it to get out of the station.

At first it might be a good idea to buy a one-day ticket (*ichinichi joshaken*). In Tokyo the Tokyo Free Pass (*Furuii Kippu*) allows you unlimited travel on all JR lines in downtown Tokyo; Toei trams, buses and subways; and Eidan subways. You can buy it at the ticket office of any JR train station, Toei subway station or major subway stations for ¥1580. In Osaka, the One Day Pass costs ¥850. You buy it at the subway stations and it gives you unlimited travel on all Osaka city subway, bus and 'newtram' (monorail) services for one day. In Kyoto the One Day Pass and Subway ticket costs ¥1200 and can be used on all city subways and buses in Kyoto.

Travelling by buses. Buses are a cheap way to get around but the hassle of using them (unless you read Japanese) makes them something of a 'locals only' form of transport. In some places, however, you might not have a choice, so here are a few tips. The final destination is usually displayed in *kanji* above the windscreen, with a route number. It's a good idea to get someone to write down your destination in *kanji*, which you can then show to the driver or another passenger so they can tell you when to get off. Buses in Nikko and Nara (popular tourist spots) have recorded announcements in English.

There are two kinds of bus:

1. Set-fare buses. Around Tokyo, Kyoto and Osaka you pay a set fare (¥200 in Tokyo and Osaka, ¥220 in Kyoto) when you get on the bus. Like an excursion fare, this lets you travel all over the city on one ticket. In Kyoto you can buy a book of tickets for buses from ¥1000 (containing ¥200 and ¥100 tickets) which you can use on city buses, Kyoto buses, Keihan buses, Kyoto Kotsu buses, Hankyu buses and JR buses. There are three types of books: ¥1000, ¥3000 and ¥5000.

2. Pay-as-you-go buses. On these buses you pay for the distance you've travelled. Get on by the rear door and take a ticket from the ticket-dispensing machine. This ticket has a number which represents the stop where you got on. When you get off, check the electric sign by the front door showing the fare for that stop, or check the fare chart by the front door and pay the amount corresponding to your ticket number. To pay you have to put the exact money into a clear plastic box beside the driver on your way out. If you get confused, enlist the help of a fellow passenger. Show them your ticket as you're getting off and say '*Sumimasen,* (destination name) *made ikura desu*' ('How much is it to ... ?').

Using the trams. Trams are as cheap as buses and trains, and being above ground it's easier than the subway to figure out where you are and which direction you're going. Fares work the same way as for buses and unlimited travel tickets are often available. The following cities operate tram services: Hiroshima and Okayama (Honshu); Nagasaki, Kumamoto and Kagoshima (Kyushu); Kochi and Matsuyama (Shikoku); and Hakodate (Hokkaido) and there's a single remaining line in both Sapporo and Tokyo. There's a service called 'newtram' in Osaka but it's actually a monorail.

Travelling by scooter. One of the best ways to get around your local area is by motor scooter: faster than a bicycle, easier to park than a car, and able to zoom past traffic jams in a single acceleration. To buy a standard 50 cc scooter second-hand, you're looking at about

¥25,000 plus ¥8000 to register it. To fill up the tiny tank, which can last a whole week, costs as little as ¥250. If the scooter is 50 cc or under you don't need a motorcycle licence, just your International Driving Permit. An advantage of scooters over 250 cc is that you can ride on freeways. Most motorists tend to be considerate of scooter riders. Helmets are required by law. One disadvantage is that scooters can be a drag in the rainy season when waterproof pants and jacket become part of your daily wardrobe.

Car travel. Whilst cars aren't so good for exploring cities in Japan (trains are faster, petrol and tolls are expensive, and traffic and parking can be a major hassle), they can be a great way to see the countryside or to get around if you decide to live outside of the major cities. Japanese drive on the left, all major road signs are in *romaji*, the roads are well maintained and the speed limit on most roads is only 40 to 50 km/h. Most cars are less than three years old because it becomes increasingly expensive to pass registration after that age. This means there are a lot of good cars for a lot less than you'd pay for them back home (I once bought a car for AUD$500 and it ran for a year!). Make sure you buy a bilingual road atlas since many rural areas don't have signs in English. To find out more about rental cars, try www.nipponrentacar.co.jp/service/general.htm.

Catching taxis. The best way to use taxis without breaking your budget, is to use them only for short distances or to find an address you're unsure of. In these cases take a train or subway to the local area and take a taxi for the last five minutes of the trip. As cabbies don't usually speak English and have a fear of the language barrier—mostly they assume you're a tourist with no knowledge of the language and are worried about how they're going to communicate the fare to you. As a result, foreigners can have trouble getting a cab. Don't take it personally.

If you're travelling alone and your Japanese isn't so good, have your destination written down in *kanji* including, if possible, a contact phone number for the place; the street layout is so weird that even taxi drivers get lost. To say 'Please take me to this address' (handing the driver the written address) say, '*Kono jusho made onegai shimasu.*'

To ask 'How much will it cost to go there?' say, *'Ryoukin wa dore gurai desu ka.'* The basic taxi fare is ¥600 for the first 2 km and ¥100 for every 370 metres after that and a timed charge if you're stuck in traffic. There's a 20% surcharge between 11 pm and 5 am.

Taxis are a little different to the ones back home. A red light on the passenger side of the windscreen means the taxi is available. There are different prices for different sized cars; the larger the cab, the higher the charge. When you flag one down you have to wait until the driver, using a lever, opens the back door on the left hand side (closest the curb). Once you're in, the door is closed automatically by the driver. There's no escape, no way you can get out without paying the ferryman. The driver will be uniformed, from cap and white gloves right down to his (or her) polished shoes. In fact, the taxi will be so immaculately clean and tidy, often complete with lace headrest covers and lace curtains and a perspex divider between you and the driver, you'll feel like you're in a limo. When you reach your destination, the driver will either write down or tell you the fare, you'll pay and the door will be opened so you can get out.

JAWHM

Once in Japan, the first port of call for any self-respecting working holiday maker should be the incredibly helpful Japan Association for Working Holiday Makers (JAWHM). The JAWHM is the only organisation in Japan specifically set up to assist working holiday makers. Although technically an 'official' organisation (it was set up by the Japanese Ministry of Labour), it's an informal non-profit organisation with English speaking staff.

The roles of the JAWHM include:

- explanation of Japanese culture, society and lifestyles
- free job referral service for working holiday makers and information about the Japanese employment scene
- general information about accommodation and homestays
- travel advice.

To use the services you first have to register (this is free) by taking your passport and two photos to any of the three JAWHM offices when you arrive in Japan (see Appendix for addresses). When you register, you are given a Working Holiday Member's Card which you should take with you every time you go there, and you'll have a 10 minute meeting with a working holiday counsellor who will give you tips on living and working in Japan. The JAWHM is open Monday to Friday, from 9.30 am to noon and 1 pm to 5.30 pm. It's closed Saturdays, Sundays, national holidays and from 29 December to 3 January.

Work-related information and general advice offered by the JAWHM includes: types of jobs available; how to find a job; information on contracts, taxes, standard rates of pay and working conditions; employee rights; and working for a Japanese company. After you register you can apply for any of the jobs on file. When you see a job you like, ask one of the staff to give you the phone number of the employer and a letter of introduction (which basically says you're a bona fide working holiday maker and have the JAWHM's blessing). You then contact the employer yourself, set up an interview and show them the letter of introduction. In 1999, JAWHM had more than 1400 positions available to working holiday makers including jobs as English teachers, waiters, hotel staff, translators, proofreaders, office workers and salespeople.

Other services include: orientation meetings, cultural exchange parties and information for Japanese working holiday makers going overseas. The JAWHM also conducts research and gathers statistics relating to the working holiday scheme to enable them to improve their services for you. From mid-2001 they will also be providing services to British working holiday makers.

Street addresses

It's almost impossible to find a house or apartment in Japan from the address alone. Only the postmen know how to do this and even they take a while to find new places (that's why when you move into a new apartment it takes a week or two to get your first mail).

Street directories do exist, in fact they're often incredibly detailed, showing not only each building but the owner's name, businesses and other information. However, unlike our street directories, they're not really used by the general public. Instead, if you have to go somewhere new, someone will usually give you detailed directions—something along the lines of: 'You know where Kentucky Fried Chicken is? Well, turn left at the next traffic lights and keep going until you come to the little cake shop on the corner, then ...' —or they'll meet you at a familiar spot and personally show you the way. It's quite the standard thing to do, even for people who have lived in the same area for years.

Addresses in Japan are written 'upside down' compared to what we're used to. They start with the largest area (country or prefecture) and work down, with the person's name at the bottom. Although sometimes, just to confuse, they'll be written the other way around.

Police

With such a confusing address system, and such a low crime rate, it's hardly surprising that one of the main functions of local police officers (*keisatsu*) is to give directions to lost citizens. They also serve as Lost and Found centres: in fact, according to the JNTO, 73% of the 2.4 billion yen in cash that was lost during 1998 was returned to its rightful owners. An amazing statistic in anyone's language.

This is not to say they don't have a crime squad or detectives. The only contact I ever had with the police, in fact, was when a group of detectives knocked on my door at 4 am one morning. Apparently a neighbour had gone missing earlier that night and they were doing the rounds of nearby houses to see if anyone had seen or heard anything. As luck would have it, I had seen a woman getting into a car with two men that night when I arrived home from work around 10 pm, so I spent half an hour explaining exactly what I'd seen. The next morning, around 10 am, there was another knock on the door. I opened it to find one of the detectives standing there holding a gift-wrapped box. He just came by, he said, to say that the woman had been found (she'd just gone walkabout for a few hours without telling her family) and to thank me for my cooperation. The gift turned out to be an assortment of exquisite little cakes. Standard procedure, you understand.

Every community has a police box (*koban*) usually on a street corner or busy intersection, which is staffed by a police officer 24 hours a day. There are about 14,500 neighbourhood police boxes and residential police stations (all called *koban*). This is how the police and the community keep in touch; you rarely see police 'on the beat' and, if they are patrolling, they're likely to do it on a bicycle. Police officers are armed but so few members of the public have guns that the police seldom use theirs. A word of advice: if you do have to ask for directions or help from a *koban*, and you've been in the country more than 90 days, make sure you're carrying your Alien Card (see below).

Alien registration

If you're going to be in Japan for more than 90 days, you must register in the town/city where you're living. Once you register, you become an official 'alien', and you're required by law to carry your Alien Card with you at all times.

How to become an alien

- Within 90 days of arriving in Japan, go to the town hall, city office or town office (check the location with someone who lives in your area). Take your passport and two passport-sized photos. You'll be given a temporary Alien Registration Card (or Alien Card) on the spot.

- You'll then have to return to the office within about two weeks to pick up your real Alien Card (*Gaikokujin toroku-sho*), which will show your name, address, birth date and how long your visa is valid, and can be used as a means of identification so you don't have to carry your passport around.

- You must carry your Alien Card with you at all times. If you're stopped by police, ask police for directions or have an accident, the first thing they'll ask for is your Alien Card. Immigration officers also have the authority to ask to see your card at any time. If you can't produce it you might be faced with a heavy fine or at least some heavy apologising and explaining which can be a time-consuming hassle.

- If you lose your Alien Card, move house, or change your name or visa status you must report this to the issuing office within 14 days.

Often while you're registering at city hall, you'll be given an English language information booklet for residents. Even the smallest city will have some kind of booklet detailing just about everything there is to know about your local area, including alien registration, paying tax, the education system, child care, health, water, sewerage and garbage services, public facilities, coping with natural disasters, and how to read your gas and electricity bills.

Phones

You'll probably want to phone home to let your family and friends know that you arrived safely. Until you get a more permanent place to lay your backpack, your link to the rest of the world will probably be a public phone.

Most public phones take coins (¥10 and ¥100) and/or phonecards, either the prepaid ones with the magnetic strip or the ones with a PIN (both of which are available at small corner stores, tobacconists and convenience stores or from a vending machine inside some phone boxes). In Tokyo they're clamping down on magnetic strip phonecards because there are so many illegal ones; best to use one with a PIN, e.g. KDD's Moshi Moshi card.

The charge for a local phone call is ¥10 per minute. A ¥1000 phonecard gives you 105 units. They also make good souvenirs: if you buy a phonecard at a tourist spot, it'll often have a photo of the local attraction on it.

International calls can be made from international public phone boxes which are green—but you'll need a prepaid phonecard or credit card since these phones don't usually take coins. These phone boxes are located at ports, airports, major hotels, major post offices and main train stations. Some international public phones have a button you can press to see instructions in English and other languages.

There are three main international access codes, one for each of the three telecommunications companies: 001 (KDD), 0041 (ITJ or Japan Telecom) and 0061 (IDC). For direct dial calls, you'll need to dial one of these codes (i.e. 001, 0041 or 0061) + country code (61 for Australia, 64 for New Zealand, 44 for the UK, 1 for Canada and the US, and 353 for Ireland) + area code (minus the zero) + local phone number. Direct dial calls can be up to 40% cheaper between 11 pm and 8 am.

A call back service allows you to call direct from any phone and find out how much your call has cost. To use this service dial 002 before the country code. When you hang up, the operator calls you back (actually it's a recorded message) to tell you, in Japanese then in English, the length of the call and the cost.

Only KDD handles reverse charge ('collect') calls: just dial 0051 from anywhere in Japan (free of charge) and ask for a collect call to the country you're calling. All the operators speak English. Beware: reverse charge calls are more expensive than direct dial calls, sometimes almost twice as much. You can also pay for your call by credit card by calling 0051. Credit cards can be used on KDD Credit Phones, KDD IC Global Phones and Japan Telecom Phones. For more information, call (toll free) KDD on 0057, Japan Telecom on 0120 44 0041 or IDC on 0120 03 0061.

There are several phonecards available in Japan that can be used to make international and domestic calls on public phones. Prepaid ones include InVox Card (available in ¥3000 or ¥5000), KDD SuperWorld Card, KDD IC Global Card and 0061 Love Love Home Card. You can also buy prepaid phonecards in your home country that allow you to make calls overseas including in Japan. Some you insert into the phone, others require you to dial a number. The latter give you the advantage of allowing you to make calls from any phone (home, work, mobile or public phones) but dialling the numbers can be time consuming: you generally have to dial in an access number, a card number, your PIN and then the international number you want to call (phew!). Some cards allow you to 'top up' the credit when you run out. Others are a fixed price allowing you to only make calls up to the prepaid value of the card. There are also cards that allow you to charge the calls you make in Japan back to an account in your home country. Check out these type of cards with telephone companies before you leave home.

Time differences. To calculate the time back home when calling from Japan, refer to the following (remember to add an hour when it's daylight saving in each of these countries—Japan doesn't have daylight saving time). For example, if it's 10 am in Japan, it's 11 am in Sydney (12 noon during daylight savings).

Auckland	+3	Dublin	−9
Sydney	+1	Toronto	−14
Adelaide	+½	Vancouver	−17
Perth	−1	New York	−14
London	−9	Los Angeles	−17

Domestic calls. Domestic codes start with a zero, e.g. 03 for Tokyo, 06 for Osaka, 075 for Kyoto and 078 for Kobe. Domestic calls are cheaper at night, on weekends and public holidays.

Email. Internet cafes are becoming more common in Japan but they're still not as widespread as they might be back home. There are currently fewer than 100 listed for Japan at www.netcafeguide.com compared to 138 Australia and 260 in the UK. If you have a Compuserve or America Online (AOL) account you can pick up your messages by calling local numbers in Japan. If you've got your own computer or mobile phone you can also plug it in to some of the grey IDD public phones.

Post offices

Japanese post offices (*yubinkyoku*) are right up there with the seventh wonder of the world. For one thing the staff understand the Japanese street layout, an incredible feat for any mere mortal. They deliver mail every day except Sunday and even throughout some public holiday periods. They read addresses written in English. You can use them as banks (see Money matters, below) and many have an automatic bill-paying service. The main post offices in each city are open long hours: usually from 9 am to 7 pm weekdays, 9 am to 5 pm Saturdays and 9 am to 12.30 pm Sundays and public holidays. Tokyo International Post Office near Tokyo station is even open 24 hours. Local post offices are generally open from 9 am to 5 pm weekdays and sometimes Saturday mornings.

Of course you can also use them to send letters home. Even in this role post offices operate on a level of service seldom encountered elsewhere. After you buy the stamps the clerk will often keep the letter and put the stamps on for you, particularly in local post offices. In any case, it's considered impolite to lick stamps—you're meant to use the sponges provided. The same goes for envelopes since most have no adhesive: seal them with sticky tape or glue, also provided at the post office. The cheapest way to write home is to buy aerograms at a cost of ¥90. Air mail generally takes four to five days to Australia and New Zealand; and five to seven days to the US, Canada and Europe.

Until you get an address, you can use the central post office in any major city as a Poste Restante. These post offices will keep any letters that have the words 'Poste Restante' under your name (usually for 30 days, after which mail is returned to the sender). When you pick up your mail, ask for either *'tome oki'* or *'kyoku dome'* and take your passport or some other identification. You can make it easier for the staff to find your letters if you ask your family and friends to use a particular coloured envelope each time they write. Every week *The Japan Times* publishes a list of names of people who have mail waiting at the Tokyo post offices.

If you want to have mail sent to you this way, give one of the following addresses to your family and friends. For cities not listed, look up the address of the main post office (*chuo yubinkyoku*) in your English Telephone Directory:
Tokyo Central Post Office, 7-2 Marunouchi 2-chome, Chiyoda-ku, Tokyo 100-8799. Tel. (03) 3284 9500.

Tokyo International Post Office, 3-3 Otemachi 2-chome, Chiyoda-ku, Tokyo 100-3199. Tel. (03) 3241 4891.

Osaka Central Post Office, 2-4 Umeda 3-chome, Kita-ku, Osaka City 530-8799. Tel. (06) 6347 8147.

Kyoto Central Post Office, 843-12 Higashi Shiokoji-cho, Shimogyo-ku, Kyoto City 600-8799. Tel. (075) 365 2555.

Nagoya Central Post Office, 1-1 Meikeki 1-chome, Nakamura-ku, Nagoya 450-8799. Tel. (052) 564 2113.

Money matters

Despite its high tech, computerised façade Japan is still a largely cash-based society, which means that even if you're working, you may not need to open a bank account. If you're going to be paid in cash, you probably won't need one; it's generally safe to keep your money under your *futon* and it's common practice to carry large wads of cash around. If your employer wants to transfer your pay directly into a bank account, however, then you will need one, preferably at your employer's bank. Personal cheques are a rarity in Japan: people either use transfers into your account or pay in cash, and many use the automatic bill-paying service many banks offer.

The best way to open a bank account is to take a Japanese friend with you to translate and help you fill out all the necessary forms. Post offices also offer banking services with the added convenience of being open longer hours than banks. You can open a savings account at your local post office, have your salary paid into it, withdraw money from any post office and pay your bills without ever having to set foot in a bank. The only thing post offices can't do is cash travellers cheques and buy or sell international currency. To open a post office account, go into your local post office and say, '*Yubin chokin no koza o tsukutte kudasai*' ('I'd like to open a post office savings account please').

Credit cards aren't as widely used in Japan as they are in other countries. The most widely accepted cards are Mastercard, Visa and American Express.

Automatic Teller Machines (ATMs) are becoming more common but they're nowhere near as convenient as back home. Few are open 24 hours, many are open only during bank hours, and most are only open between 8 am and 9 or 10 pm. The exceptions are the ATMs of major international banks such as Citibank, which are generally open 24 hours a day and accept major credit cards.

Visitors to Japan can also withdraw cash from 8000 Japanese post office ATMs using credit cards issued overseas and JCB cards. In March 2001 the number of ATMs offering this service increased to 21,000 (80% of all Japanese post office ATMs).

Name stamp

A *hanko* or name stamp is the Japanese equivalent of a signature, particularly for official documents. Most people have a specific kind of *hanko* called an *inkan* which must be registered as your official 'signature' at the local city office. They're usually made of wood (they used to be made of ivory) and have your name in *kanji* or, in the case of *gaijin*, *kanji* or *katakana* characters close to the syllables in your name. They can cost anything from ¥500 for the most basic up to ¥200,000 for one made from more expensive materials but they're usually around ¥1500, plus ¥300 to register it at the city hall.

Hanko are convenient if you need someone else to do your banking or to 'sign' some official document for you. No-one seems too concerned about the risk of someone stealing your *hanko* and using it for less than helpful purposes (like draining your bank account). If you don't want to get a *hanko* or *inkan*, banks and post offices will still accept a signature but be prepared to fit your signature into a tiny space about one centimetre square. You can use your initials instead of your full name to get around this, but make sure you always sign the same way. Banks prefer you to have a *hanko* and some banks even offer to get one made for you free of charge. The disadvantage of using your 'sign' (as they call a handwritten signature) is that you can only withdraw money at the branch of the bank where you opened your account. If you go to another branch, they have to obtain a faxed copy of your 'sign' from your original bank.

Living

Japan—where the living is easy

Easy? Japan? A country of 127 million people, whose customs and whole philosophy are so different to the ones you were brought up with. A place where you can't understand the TV, radio, or announcements on the train that tell you it doesn't stop at your station. Where it takes years of study just to be able to read a newspaper and you have to carry an Alien Card wherever you go and be called a *gaijin*, even if you've lived there for years. It may be hard to believe, but once you've become accustomed to being conspicuous and being asked how old you are by complete strangers, Japan is a very user-friendly country.

Let's get the hassles out of the way first. It's true that Japan can be frustrating, particularly for the newly arrived. There are the inevitable things that accompany a move to any new country—like homesickness, strange food and different ways of doing things. The sheer size of Japanese cities and the reality of living with less personal space can take some getting used to. And it can be mentally tiring when you don't understand the language, and simple tasks like getting a plug for your hair dryer can require all your powers of ingenuity.

The first month or so I spent in Japan I craved bread: good, wholesome, three-grain-with-kibbles bread, not the sweet white six-slice loaves they sell in Japanese supermarkets. Living in a rural area I felt cut off from the outside world. I didn't know where to buy English language books or magazines and I'd exhausted all the ones I'd brought with me. I didn't read a newspaper or listen to the news for weeks on end and I couldn't even read the local telephone book. Worst of all, I didn't know anyone well enough to talk to about all those 'not-really-happy-to-be-here' feelings.

Those feelings did pass, however, and I came to realise that Japan caters for foreigners like no other country. There are English language newspapers and magazines, bilingual TV and radio stations,

English language telephone directories, even English-speaking travel agents and doctors servicing foreign residents. Most cities have at least one international centre providing free Japanese language lessons and newspapers, books and videos in various languages. Local libraries often stock some English language fiction and non-fiction books and magazines. Then there are the cinemas—almost all movies are shown in English with Japanese subtitles—and all video stores stock movies in English.

In fact, Japan is becoming so Westernised that you can find almost anything you miss from home. There are Western-style family restaurants with names like Royal Host and Ninjin Boy, European bakeries that sell baguettes and French cake shops. More and more department stores are stocking imported foods (for a price). The latest fashions are easy to find as long as your size is not too different to Japanese sizes.

If you wanted to, you could even fool yourself into believing you'd never left the English-speaking world. Besides teaching English, you could hang out with *gaijin* and Japanese people who want to improve their English. There are English words on shops, drink cans, clothes, cars and food packaging. Not all of which make sense: I once bought a pad of writing paper that had emblazoned across its cover 'If there is changing beauty there is constant beauty. Enjoy lasting pleasure and satisfaction in using this report pad'. If this doesn't make life any easier, at least it keeps things interesting.

Teaching English is a real 'welcome mat' to the culture too. You spend so much time talking to your students, particularly in conversation classes, that teaching becomes a two-way learning process: while they're learning English, you're learning about the country and its people. The conversations can cover a wide range of topics, largely because of the wide variety of students. My students have included a Korean-born rock singer, a jet fighter pilot, an 81-year-old woman who survived the Hiroshima atomic bomb, a class of scuba divers and kids as young as five (from whom I learned *origami*!), as well as the more usual housewives, high school students and office workers. It's also not unusual for students to invite their teachers home for a meal or to some other social outing, which gives you another 'in' to the culture.

In Japan, the customer is king, which makes basic chores like shopping easier than back home. Doors to even the smallest shops magically glide open when you approach. Supermarket trolleys are designed so that all four wheels go in the same direction! There are 24-hour takeaway food shops and most city shops are open well into the night, particularly on Fridays and Saturdays. The shopping itself is quick and simple when you can't read the labels—instead of checking the contents, just look for one word (like 'shampoo') or check the picture on the pack. If you've just got home from work and can't raise yourself off the *tatami* mat to cook or eat out, you can always ring the local restaurant and your dinner will be delivered on a china plate with utensils. Even the local liquor shops will home-deliver.

When Kobe was hit by the massive earthquake which killed more than 5000 people in January 1995, foreign correspondents reported that residents and even injured victims dealt with the crisis with an otherworldly sense of calm. But it's not just in a crisis that people act this way in Japan. Interpersonal harmony is a way of life. People tend to obey rules, show respect for authority and treat each other according to social guidelines, all of which does much to reduce the stress of living so close together.

It's an easy country to live in ... the day-to-day living is very easy. You don't really have to think that much, you don't have to worry about all that much. People really go out of their way to help you and that's nice. People kind of go with the flow ... there's no real disturbance, there's no real confrontation ... you don't have to worry about people getting upset with you ... which makes it a little more harmonious than America. Alda Borror

It's a cakewalk. You can come here and it's such an easy place to be. People really enjoy helping other people, it gives them a real sense of satisfaction. Peter Moses

On another level, living in any foreign country has advantages that you often don't see until you leave your house or apartment. Life becomes simpler when your head space isn't cluttered with advertising and media messages. As an 'outsider' you live beyond Japan's own social rules: *gaijin* are expected to be a little weird, and you're given plenty of rope regarding what is acceptable behaviour. The short working week gives you more free time than you ever had back home: time to be creative, to study, or take up new interests. All of which makes for a very free existence. Within reason, Japan can be a really easy place to just be yourself, follow your own rhythms and keep life simple.

English language media

Considering less than 1% of its population is foreign, Japan has an impressive array of English language media.

English language telephone directories. These could well be your most valuable source of information. In addition to the normal stuff found in telephone books, the Townpage English Telephone Directories (published by NTT) contain contact details for virtually everything the foreign resident could ever want or need including English–speaking doctors, dentists and travel agents; hospitals with English speaking staff; English conversation schools and other potential employers and employment agencies in your area; emergency phone numbers; and embassies and consulates. They also provide subway maps, sightseeing tips and city tourist maps; information on postal services and utilities (water, electricity and gas); and listings of festivals, international events and public holidays.

There are two annual editions. The East Japan edition covers everywhere north of Tokyo while the West Japan edition is for the south. The local directory is free to residents but there is a ¥2000 fee for additional copies or for a copy of the other directory. Visit your local NTT office (Japan's main telecommunications company) or phone the English Townpage Centre in Tokyo on (03) 3459 7511. You can also access all the information in the directories or order one via the website: english.itp.ne.jp/

Newspapers and news magazines. There are several quality English language newspapers, all produced in Tokyo. The main ones are *The Japan Times, The Daily Yomiuri, The Mainichi Daily News* and *The Asahi Evening News*. Since they are produced exclusively for foreign residents they contain useful up-to-date information you couldn't find elsewhere. This includes exchange rates, the latest international airfares (and advertisements for English–speaking travel agents), overseas news items and entertainment listings, as well as classified ads placed by other *gaijin*.

You can also get foreign news magazines such as *Time* and *Newsweek* but expect to pay up to four times more than you would back home. For foreigners wanting to practise their Japanese reading skills, there are newspapers in simple Japanese, such as the *Hiragana Times* and the *Nihongo Journal*.

Foreigners' magazines are the best sources of information about what's on in your city—parties, movies, concerts, gigs—as well as feature articles about living in Japan, Japanese culture and travelling around Japan. Most have classifieds with sections on employment, accommodation and items for sale. The main foreigners' magazines are *Tokyo Time Out*, *Tokyo Journal*, *Tokyo Notice Board*, *Kansai Time Out* and *Kansai Flea Market* (Kansai is the area around Osaka, Kobe and Kyoto), *Eyes* (in Nagoya), *The Alien* (Nagoya, Kansai, Tokyo) and *Metro* (Fukuoka).

Bookshops selling English language books are worth visiting to pick up a bilingual Japan atlas, or perhaps a bilingual map of your city and prefecture. The main ones are: Kinokuniya (www.kinokuniya.co.jp) with 60 stores throughout Japan and 26 overseas stores including in Los Angeles, New York, San Francisco and Sydney; Maruzen with more than 37 stores in Japan; as well as Asahiya and Sanseido.

English TV. You can buy stereo TV sets which let you watch certain programs in Japanese or the original language (the language the program was made in). Tokyo has five commercial TV stations plus NHK, the national TV station, which broadcasts a bilingual news program every weeknight (the simultaneous translation is impressive, but it's hardly world news—for that you're better off listening to the BBC World Service or other overseas radio broadcast). The English language TV programs aren't usually of a very high calibre but if you don't mind watching repeats of those old American sit-coms you grew up with and movies at 2 am (when the English language movies are usually shown), it's cheap entertainment. What the heck, at least it's in English and it's been months since you've seen anything on the box in your own language. That was my excuse, anyway, when sprung watching repeats of *Little House on the Prairie* on my days off.

Japanese TV shows range from every kind of game show under the rising sun to 'That's Incredible' video showcases, soap operas and dramas. There's something for every TV junkie and it's a great way to practise your Japanese comprehension skills.

Most *gaijin* go for the satellite TV option if they're staying awhile. There are two free-to-air satellite channels: NHKS-1 (or BS-7) and NHKS-2 (BS-11) but you'll need a satellite dish. Sometimes the apartment block you live in or your workplace will have one (many English conversation schools use broadcast English programs as teaching material). Otherwise you'll have to fork out about ¥8000 to buy your own. There are also pay-to-view channels such as WOWOW (BS-5), CNN International and BBC World. These cost about ¥27,000 for connection and about ¥3000 per month.

Videos. Renting a new release video overnight costs about ¥500 while weekly rentals cost about ¥400. If you want to watch videos you've brought from home, remember that Japan uses the NTSC format used in the US and Canada, so PAL and SECAM tapes from Australia, New Zealand or European countries will have to be converted (some international centres do this for a small fee); otherwise make sure you get a VCR that plays both kinds.

Radio. BYO favourite music and a discman! Japanese radio stations are notoriously 'poppy', and after the novelty of listening to Japanese DJs wears off you'll find yourself unable to get those inane Japanese pop tunes out of your head. Better to invest in a discman or MD player and take your favourite discs. Ask friends back home to record a couple of hours of your favourite radio station and send the tape. The following Japanese radio stations have at least some programs in English: NHK-FM (82.5 MHz), Tokyo FM (80.0 MHz), InterFM (76.1 MHz), J-Wave (FM Japan – 81.3 MHz), Yokohama Radio (84.7 MHz), FM CoCoLo in Osaka (76.5 MHz), as well as the FEN (Far East Network) run by the US Armed Services stationed in Okinawa. There are also short wave English radio stations, most notably BBC World Service and Voice of America.

Deciding where to live

What's important to you? Do you want to be in the heart of a big city, in a rural area or in the mountains? Do you want to live where you make good money or is lifestyle more important? Perhaps you want to study a martial art, have time to draw or paint, immerse yourself in your city's music and club scene, or go snowboarding/surfing/hiking on your days off. Here are a few things to consider when making your decision.

Travelling around Japan and getting a feel for different places before you settle into a work routine can give you an insight into the country. My first visit to Japan was a reconnaissance mission as much as a holiday: I wanted to have a good look around the country to see if there was somewhere I'd really like to live for a while. And there was. It was a small town (population about 2000) on the coast of southern Kyushu, with a few pretty beaches nearby and good surf. There were even two friendly *gaijin* living there. When I returned to Australia, I decided I'd love to try living there and I thought about this little dot on the map for two years while planning my escape from Sydney. When I finally returned, there was no work there (so that's why there were only two *gaijin* in such a beautiful place!), so I decided to try the next big settlement, Miyazaki, about 50 km away. I had a car, so driving back to my favourite spot wouldn't be hard. I soon picked up a few hours teaching, found a temporary place to stay, got to know a few locals and that was it, I had a new home.

Tokyo, Osaka and Nagoya offer more work opportunities with better pay than smaller cities and towns. They also have more nightlife, foreign food, *gaijin* and English language resources. People tend to be more open-minded and accepting of different cultures. In any major city many of your Japanese friends will probably speak English, which can be good or bad depending on whether or not you want to learn Japanese. Some of the disadvantages of big cities include the high cost of living (especially if you live close to the centre), the constant pressures of crowding, the noise and the pollution.

Living in a small to medium sized city or town can be good for your Japanese and cheaper than a big city while giving you the chance to experience a more traditional Japan. Bear in mind that it can be more of a culture shock than living in a big metropolis. In the some out-of-the-way places you might even have to do without a TV and cinema.

You have to make up your mind if you want to live in a city of that magnitude [Tokyo or Osaka] and have the experience of that. A lot of Americans who go to Japan have more experience than the average Aussie or Kiwi of living in large metropolises. It also depends on how much you feel you want to be part of the expatriate community and if you like music or the nightlife scene. And if you like nature, but even if you live in a city it's not that far out, it's only an hour or two by train to get to some reasonable nature. Fukuoka [in northern Kyushu] seems to be the place in many ways: it's big enough to have quite a lot of work, it's small enough that you can get out and be in really nice places within an hour or so, plus you've got the rest of Kyushu to play in. It's got an international airport. It's also very cosmopolitan. It's got a lot of good restaurants, foreign restaurants, there's quite a large and diverse population. It's not so huge that it's hard to get around. It's probably not all that cheap to live there though. Another thing to think about is that you might hate being in Japan. It's probably a little easier to leave a city than a country area where you've had to spend more time setting yourself up. Stewart Clark

Living in a tourist city like Kyoto or Nara can be more of a cultural experience, but you have to contend with large numbers of tourists in the main city areas, particularly at peak times, and plenty of other foreigners (which means either a supportive or competitive work environment, depending on how you see it).

Tokyo was a bit gaijin-ed out. I chose Osaka because there were fewer foreigners, and it's close to Kyoto, with its temples and peace and quiet, and Nara, which has a really nice park with deer as well as its temples. Jess Halford

Close to other *gaijin* or not? While you may feel that living too close to other *gaijin* takes away from the experience of living in any foreign country, it can have advantages. Foreigners tend to help each other out, for one thing—which comes in handy when you're looking for work or a place to live, or even for furniture for your new abode. Living in a *gaijin*-rich area can also mean that your Japanese neighbours will be used to seeing foreigners and won't freak out when you walk into the local supermarket.

The weather can affect where you choose to live too. Kyoto, for instance, is renowned for its blistering summers and snow-coated winters. The far north and south of the country have extremes of weather, such as −20°C in Hokkaido's bleak winter and typhoons slamming into Okinawa and the southern islands in late summer.

Accommodation options

Gaijin **houses or guest houses.** These are apartment blocks that have been leased by someone (usually a *gaijin*) who rents out individual rooms or apartments to *gaijin* at slightly higher rents than normal. They're usually only found in the major cities where there is a high turnover of *gaijin*. Flexibility is the main advantage: you can move in straight away, stay for short periods (the minimum is usually a week), and only have to give a few weeks' notice when you want to move out. You also don't have the hassle of paying a bond or 'key money' (see Renting apartments below).

Living arrangements at *gaijin* houses are usually communal—you'll share a dining room, kitchen and bathroom—plus you might have access to English newspapers, the internet, a bilingual TV and other facilities, not to mention plenty of other foreigners to talk to (and find things out from). Rents start at around ¥2200 per night, ¥14,000 per week or ¥55,000 per month for a single room. To find *gaijin* houses in your city, ask at the local international centre, check the foreigners' magazines/newspapers or ask at the Japan Association for Working Holiday Makers.

'NO KEY MONEY. Guest houses. Clean and convenient. 24 hour free internet access. BANANA HOUSE (large private room with A/C, video room, coin laundry, many common rooms, sauna, free shower & utilities), Mozuhiman stn. (Nankai Koya line, to Namba) and Mozu stn. (JR Hanwa line to Tennoji). Nakamozu stn. (subway Midosuji line). There is a special rent for long-term guest. Weekly ¥15,500 upward. Monthly ¥55,000 upward. We have CABLE TV (CNN, MTV, movies, sports, etc). We also have private apartments in Namba. Call for more details at 06-6627-0790 or 0722-59-7385. Web page www.oct.zaq.ne.jp/orange/.' *Kansai Time Out*

Renting apartments (*apaato*) and houses (*ie*). If you're thinking about renting an apartment on your own, be prepared to pay anything from ¥45,000 per month for a small place (with bathroom and kitchen) about 20 minutes subway ride from the city centre, up to ¥70,000 or ¥80,000 per month for a one room studio in the heart of the city (Tokyo will be the most expensive, followed closely by Osaka, with other smaller cities such as Nagoya and Fukuoka being cheaper still).

There are various kinds of apartments: from *mansion* at the top end to modern apartment blocks (called 'condos') to *danchi*, which are cheap functional public flats at the bottom end. A house will be more spacious but also more expensive than an apartment; also they're usually at least a 30 minute train ride from the city centre.

No matter what kind of dwelling you choose, however, you should be prepared for some of the hassles of renting a place:

- 'Key money' is the biggest hurdle you'll face. Basically the term refers to the fees paid to the landlord and estate agent before you can move in. It can be the equivalent of up to six months rent, broken down as follows: *reikin*, a non-refundable gift to the landlord, usually two months rent; *tesuryo*, the real estate agent's commission, also non-refundable, about one month's rent; *shikikin*, equivalent to a bond, usually two months rent and refundable when you move out provided there is no damage; *tetsukekin*, a 'seal the contract' fee that goes to the landlord but is sometimes waived; and *maekin*, your first months rent (at last!). It's common practice for the rent to go up every time the annual lease is renewed. When you want to leave, you should give at least one month's notice or you could lose another month's rent.

Haggling for a reduction in key money can sometimes work, particularly in rural areas where there's less demand for accommodation. I knew an Australian couple who had their eye on an old house near the beach in southern Kyushu. It hadn't been lived in for six years, which meant it needed major cleaning. A large part of the landlord's and agent's fees goes to cleaning, fumigating and changing the *tatami* mats, so my friends offered to clean the place themselves in return for a discount on the key money. Since there were no other tenants on the horizon, the agent agreed and they got a four room house with a huge garden for a mere ¥30,000 a month. Bargain!

- Leases are generally for a minimum of one year. Shorter-term leases are almost impossible to get. In any case, once you see how much you have to pay in up-front fees, you'll want to stay for at least a year, just to get your money's worth.

- Japanese landlords and real estate agents can be somewhat reluctant to deal with *gaijin*, thanks to the urban myth that every foreigner is the 'tenant from hell', i.e. someone likely to have loud parties every night, be rude to neighbours, never pay the rent on time and trash the place when the lease is up. At the very least you'll need a Japanese person to act as your guarantor when applying and to help you communicate with the estate agent and translate the documents you'll be required to sign.

Share accommodation isn't as common as it is back home, but it's out there—though you're more likely to find a foreign flatmate (called 'room mate' or 'share mate' in Japan) than a Japanese one. The trick is to find someone who has already forked out the key money—someone on a work visa is most likely to have made the commitment required of a lease. Alternatively, you might find a *gaijin* wanting to leave Japan before their lease expires, so you can take over the apartment without the up-front fees. Or someone who's going home for a month or two and needs a housesitter while they're away.

'SHARE MATE WANTED. Ibaraki-shi. 5 min Monorail, 20 min Hankyu, 30 min JR. ¥40,000/m + utility. Call Ken 090-1919-8680. Take care Bjorn!' *Kansai Time Out*

Subsidised accommodation. Some English schools have accommodation for their teachers (often on a pay-by-the-month basis) or you might hear of a school-owned apartment that's been sitting empty for a couple of months. Sometimes an employer will even pay your key money for you, but this is generally for sponsored (i.e. work visa) employees, not those on working holiday visas.

Where to look for accommodation

Accommodation classifieds in English language publications are your best bet. Try *Kansai Time Out, Tokyo Time Out, Tokyo Classifieds, Kyoto Visitors Guide* and *Kansai Flea Market*. *The Japan Times* on Fridays and *The Daily Yomiuri* 'Reader-to-Reader Market' on Wednesdays also have accommodation classifieds but these tend to be for more upmarket (and more expensive) places. Most ads are for foreigners wanting to pass on their apartments or sublet to other *gaijin* whilst they're on summer holidays; and for *gaijin*/guest houses.

'Available 3LDK. 5 minutes to Shin-Osaka station. ¥60,000/55,000/month. Utilities included. Fully furnished. Air-conditioner. No key money. 06-6350-9570/090-4281-9783. Leave messages for Miho.' *Kansai Time Out*

'Sublet July 26th – August 27th. Fully furnished room in Nakano. Shimbashi (Marunouchi line) ¥65,000. Share with 3 others. Call 090-9815-0616.' *Tokyo Notice Board*

'BIG WORLD 21 opening special 20% off! ¥1250-3000/day. ¥28,500-46,800/month. TV, VCR, phone, fridge, A/C, etc. Musashi-Koganei station (JR Chuo line). Tel. 0422-51-2277. Fax 0422-51-4499.' *Tokyo Notice Board*

You might even find someone who's leaving Japan and wants to off-load their apartment, furniture and private English students all in one hit! The Japan Association for Working Holiday Makers (JAWHM) can also help you find a place to live (see Appendix for contact details).

Websites. There are so many websites for foreigners living in Japan, some of which are listed in this book. Do a search on 'live in Japan' or start with one of the big sites such as Tokyo Classifieds, a weekly e-zine with a huge accommodation section at www.tokyoclassified.com/.

A typical apartment

When looking for your very own apartment you won't find them advertised by the number of bedrooms. Instead, the Japanese use a system incorporating living and dining rooms and kitchen: L = living room, D = dining room, K = kitchen (usually all three are combined) and UB = unit bath (combined shower/bath/toilet in a prefabricated cubicle).

So you hear of 1LDK apartments (the smallest you can get, adequate for a single person living alone) which have one room that doubles as a dining/living room and a bedroom (when you unroll your futon), and a kitchen (usually squeezed into the hallway between the front door and the main room). A 2LDK will have two living rooms which can double as bedrooms, as well as a combined dining room/kitchen. The room size is given in terms of the number of standard size *tatami* mats (even if the flooring isn't *tatami*). One standard *tatami* mat (one *jo*) is about 1.8 x 0.9 m (1.62 m²). Most rooms are six *jo* (six mats) but there are also three, four and a half, five, eight and ten mat rooms in some apartments and houses.

You're moving in, but moving in to what? If you're going to be living in a Japanese-style place, here's what to expect from your 1LDK or 2LDK apartment:

- The front door, with mail slot, is likely to be heavy, often metal. As you go in, you'll notice a small step immediately in front of you. Leave your shoes on the lower level before stepping up into the main area of the apartment. So the walls really are made of paper! Traditional internal walls and sliding doors are made of lightweight wooden frames with either cloth or paper stretched over them. The paper doors are called *shoji*. The walls between apartments are not much thicker, usually just a thin plaster, hence the necessity to consider your neighbours at all times.

- Windows are usually sliding glass doors. A 1LDK probably won't have any windows as such, just these sliding doors opening onto a small verandah (for hanging out the washing and airing your *futon*). The doors are usually opaque at the bottom for privacy. Since virtually everything happens on the floor in a Japanese apartment, the door has to hide the view through the lower half while letting in light from the top half.

- Insulation is lacking in most places. That's probably one reason why the Japanese seem ultra-skilled at building houses and apartment blocks in record time (a legacy of the post-war years when they had to house millions of people quickly). So it makes sense to invest in an air-conditioner (reverse cycle so you have a heater in winter), particularly if you'll be spending a lot of time at home.

- Lighting for most rooms is a circular fluorescent tube in the centre of the ceiling with a pull cord that lets you change settings from (1) blindingly bright fluoro to (2) bright fluoro or (3) orange mood lighting. Waking up in the middle of the night and switching through those first two settings to find the mellow one is not fun, so think about getting a lower wattage plug-in lamp to keep by your *futon*.

- *Tatami* rooms are common in most apartments, particularly small ones where space is at a premium (the reasoning being that it's easier to rent a small *tatami* place where you can sleep on the floor than a small Western-style place which will need furnishings). Some larger Western-style apartments and houses will have at least one *tatami* room. If it's a new lease, you'll be blessed with new *tatami* mats with their fresh straw smell.

- The kitchen is usually nestled into one side of the hallway and it'll be fairly basic by Western standards. Most tenants have to supply their own fridge (about the size of a bar fridge) and a portable (don't ask me why) two-burner gas cooktop. Ovens are a rarity since traditional Japanese cooking doesn't involve much baking. The bench top will probably be a little lower than you're used to, and crowded with a host of appliances including a toaster oven, rice cooker and kettle or hot water urn. Some people have a rice cabinet in their kitchens, if they can fit one in. These are purpose-built bins for storing up to 10 kg of rice with a dispenser to measure out the required amount of rice per person.

- Most apartments now have baths (*o-furo*), but it wasn't so long ago that people used to visit the local bathhouse (*sento*) for their daily wash. Bathrooms in most houses and apartments consist of a shower, bath, toilet and hand basin all contained in one splashable room. When you go in and close the door, the bathroom becomes the shower cubicle and everything gets wet, so you need to leave your towels on a hook outside the bathroom. Most places have showers but many are low on the wall so you can wash while sitting on a low stool. In some older houses, particularly those outside the main cities, there won't be any hot running water so to have a hot bath you have to fill the bath with cold water, light the gas heater and wait 15 minutes for the water to be heated. When you've had your bath, you cover it with the vinyl cover to keep the water hot for the next person.

- In a 1LDK, the living room is literally where one does all one's living—you eat, entertain and sleep there. There might be an alcove for a shrine. One wall will probably be taken up with built-in cupboards which have fabric-covered sliding doors and one wide shelf, about waist-high, for storing *futons*. It's becoming more common to find built-in hanging space for clothes but if your apartment doesn't have any, you'll need to get a separate clothes rack or cupboard.

- Your typical monthly expenses could run something like this: rent – ¥50,000, utilities – ¥7000 – 8000, phone (no overseas calls) – ¥3000 – 4000, food – ¥30,000 – 40,000, entertainment – ¥20,000 – 30,000, transport to and from work (by bus) – ¥400 – 500, monthly internet access – ¥2000, newspaper subscription – ¥2650 (*The Daily Yomiuri*), health club membership – ¥12,000 (after a ¥10,000 sign-up fee).

Keeping in touch

It goes without saying that in order to find work you're going to need a contact phone number. The two main options for keeping in touch and being contactable are: a regular phone line and a mobile phone. Mobile phones are fast becoming the phone of choice in Japan, and not just for temporary residents like you and me.

According to the Work In Japan website (www.workinjapan.com), as of March 2000 more people have mobile telephones in Japan than land-based telephones. Not only that but more people are accessing the internet via their mobiles, given the high costs of buying a regular phone line and computer. I've even heard that in the next 10 years or so, Japan is thinking of phasing out fixed phone lines altogether.

Getting a phone line. You might move in to a place that already has the phone on, but this isn't as likely as it is back home—when people move house in Japan they not only take their number with them but the handset and the whole line (which belongs to them until they cancel it). When you get a phone in Japan the usual procedure is to buy a phone line and an accompanying number. It's like registering a car; when you want to sell that phone number to someone else you have to change the name on the line at the local NTT office (for a fee of about ¥800). The advantage of buying a phone line is that you can take your phone line and number anywhere in Japan—although this is no longer such an advantage with mobile phones now being so affordable. If you prefer this kind of set up, here's what you'll be paying:

- The initial outlay is about ¥80,000 (this includes connection, subscription to the phone service and consumption tax), plus an installation fee (around ¥2000) and administration charges (about ¥1000), though there are companies that buy and sell cheaper phone lines. The best way to get rid of your phone line when you leave Japan is to sell it to another *gaijin* (advertise in the foreigners' press).

- Phone (handset) rental costs around ¥2000 – ¥3000 per month plus any extra charges, e.g. for a push-button phone (¥250 per month) or an itemised bill (¥250 per month).

- Local calls cost about ¥10 per minute (less at night). The rate is reduced by 40% if you're calling places 60 km to 320 km away. For overseas calls, the rates are more competitive if you're calling the US or the UK than if you're calling Australia or New Zealand. Your international phone bills will be issued by whichever international carrier you've used for your calls (KDD,

ITJ or IDC). All the phone companies seem to have some kind of billing arrangement because if you don't pay your international phone bill, NTT (the national telecommunications company) will cut off your phone.

Getting a mobile phone. Prepaid mobile phones are the way to go. There's an initial outlay of ¥10,000 for the handset and three prepaid cards worth ¥1000 each. You don't need to sign up to a calling plan or pay any monthly fees or bills. You can use the phone for up to three months, after which you can throw it away (ah, the disposable society). These kinds of mobiles are available from NTT DoCoMo (check your English telephone directory for contact numbers).

Other options. Pocket Bells (pagers) are also handy to have. You usually have to pay an initial fee of ¥10,000, then ¥2000 per month. The battery costs of ¥180. You can buy a Pocket Bell from NTT DoCoMo or mobile phone shops.

Furnishing your apartment

Most, if not all, rented apartments in Japan are unfurnished. But if you decide to live in a Japanese-style place (i.e. one with *tatami* flooring) you won't need much in the way of furnishings, just a low table, some flat cushions, maybe a couple of legless chairs (really) and possibly a clothes cabinet or rack. You'll need more if you want to live in the manner to which you've become accustomed (i.e. if you're renting a Western-style apartment with carpet or hard floors) but even then finding affordable furniture won't be too much of a hassle. In fact it might well be the easiest and cheapest part of setting up house in Japan.

- 'Sayonara sales' are usually from late March to July when most foreign teachers' contracts are finishing and people are leaving.

- Check the classified sections in English language newspapers and magazines. Some classifieds even have a 'Giveaway' section—yes in the ultimate disposable society secondhand goods are so worthless, people can't sell them and actually advertise for someone to take them off their hands.

'Leaving Sept 26. Fridge, TV and VCR (bilingual), heaters, fan, low table, bookcase, free washing machine. Kyoto 090-7533-9251.' *Kansai Time Out* under 'For Sale, Sayonara'.

'Shijo-Omiya. Leaving end Sept. Phone line ¥45,000, refrigerator, washer, aircon, cordless answer phone, mountain bike, etc. 075-802-5495 (Mary).' *Kansai Time Out* under 'For Sale, Sayonara'.

- *Gomi*. Many a *gaijin* has made the claim of having furnished their entire apartment from rubbish piles (*gomi*) by the side of the road. To the uninitiated it might sound odd (even sad) but the reality is that you can find quality fridges, cooktops, rice cookers, chairs and bikes—the list is endless and most items don't need any repairs or even cleaning. It's quite acceptable to take things from *gomi*, in fact in some areas it's so much the done thing that you have to be quick to pick up the choice items. It's not like picking through the garbage tip back home—in Japan, people simply take the items straight from their home (most items are thrown away because people want to upgrade to a newer model and don't have enough storage space to keep more than one of anything) and place it by the side of the road on certain days of the month. In fact it's not uncommon for people to put such 'big garbage' items out on the street in the hope that someone like you will take them home.

- Flea markets are a good source of furniture and utensils. See English language magazines for dates and locations.

- Word of mouth. Put the word out among your Japanese and *gaijin* friends that you need a table, a rice cooker, or whatever. The chances are someone will have one of what you need to give away or they may be able to lend you things if you're only planning a short stay.

- Second-hand stores do exist in some areas. Ask friends or the police (go to the police box) for the nearest one.

- Department stores. Contrary to popular belief there are bargains to be had in some department stores. The cheaper ones are Daiei, Nafco, Best (electrical) and Handsman (hardware).

Bear in mind that if you live near the city centre you may not have to cook a meal the entire time you're in Japan since eating out is cheap (e.g. ¥650 for a bowl of noodles or a set meal with rice, beef and salad), healthy and convenient. Also, if you're teaching English you might not be getting home until 10 pm. If you do want to cook, pots and pans, ceramic or enamel bowls and chopsticks can be found in any large supermarket.

Western-style beds are available, but they can be expensive and a hassle to transport, and anyway, when in Rome ... Most Japanese sleep on a *futon* laid on the floor. A Japanese *futon* is a bit different to what we understand as a *futon*. Your entire bedding kit will consist of: a mattress (this is the real *futon*, called a *shiki-buton*), a quilt which you put on top of you (the top *futon*, called a *kake-buton*), a pillow, a quilt cover and a bottom sheet. Japanese pillows are traditionally filled with rice husks, making them like small bean bags which play havoc with delicate foreigner's necks, so it's best to go for a Western-style pillow. Cheap department stores are the best place to get bedding. You're usually looking at up to ¥8000 for a mattress *futon* and ¥5000 for the quilt.

Most Japanese appliances are smaller than we're used to—vacuum cleaners, fridges, low shelving units—all in the name of saving space. If your apartment doesn't have a washing machine, it'll be cheaper to use the local laundromat than forking out for your own machine. If you do decide to get one, you can often find old ones in the *gomi*—like the old twin tub version I had (one side washes, one side spins, no electronic parts to break). Other appliances you might want to consider include the following.

- A bilingual TV, will help you familiarise yourself with the language, allow you access to weather forecasts (remember those typhoons, earthquakes and tidal waves) and the NHK bilingual news.

- No TV is complete in Japan without its VCR, so much so that they're often built into the TV sets. Going to the cinema can be pricey, and in rural areas the local video shop can be your only chance of a nightlife.

- You'll need a heater if you plan to spend a winter anywhere but Okinawa or one of the other tropical southern islands. Confusingly, heaters are called stoves (*sutobu*) and are electric, gas or kerosene. If you want gas, you'll have to check what type (6B, 13A or propane) is connected to your apartment. You might also think about getting an electric heater (*kotatsu*) that attaches to the underside of your low table. This special kind of table also has a removable surface, so that you can put a quilt under the table top and over your legs to keep your knees and feet toasty.

A word about garbage/rubbish/trash. The Japanese were world leaders when they started separating their garbage and recycling back in the 1970s. These days they're not so far ahead of the rest of the world but they do have a few unique systems in place. Basically everything you'll be throwing out will fit into one of the following categories, which you'll put out for collection on the appropriate day.

- Burnables include anything that won't give off toxic gases when burned, usually paper and food scraps.
- Non-burnables are mostly plastics; reduce packaging as much as you can when shopping as these take up the limited space allocated for land fills in Japan.
- Recyclables include glass and plastic bottles, cardboard, newspapers, as well as metal, cloth, batteries (collected every few months) and polystyrene takeaway food containers.
- 'Big garbage' (*gomi*) are the things you want to get rid of that are too big to fit in the normal garbage truck. And remember: one persons's *gomi* is another person's means to furnish an apartment.

Shopping

The first thing you'll notice about shopping in Japan is the politeness of the staff. You'll walk in and every employee who crosses your path will greet you with '*Irasshaimase*!' ('Welcome!'). At first it seems only good manners to acknowledge them by saying hello or giving them a nod, but you soon learn that if you did this every time in every store you'd never get out. Judging from what the Japanese do, the best response is to smile at the staff but otherwise ignore them. When checking prices, remember that the 5% sales tax is added to most things at the cash register (i.e. it's not usually included in the marked price).

The best places to shop for food, in terms of value for money and the range of products, are big supermarkets and the basement food sections of most large department stores, e.g. Daimaru, Hankyu, BonBelta and Kotobukiya. Most shops are closed one day a week, usually a weekday; on other days they'll discount certain perishable items, such as fruit and bread, in the hour or so before closing time. And remember that your fridge will be tiny by Western standards, so you'll need to shop for food frequently and buy small quantities (particularly in summer when fruit will spoil rapidly in the heat). To increase your repertoire of dishes, ask a Japanese friend to shop with you once or twice and point out what certain foods are and how to prepare them. Some things to be aware of:

- Rice is not as cheap as you'd expect given that most people eat it at every meal. Japanese rice (preferred by 99.9% of Japanese households) costs about ¥1700 for a 3 kg bag (which lasts two people about two weeks). Foreign rice, often from Thailand and Australia, tends to be cheaper and just as good (in my humble *gaijin* opinion). Brown rice is not so popular and can be hard to find.

- The fish section of most supermarkets is huge—equivalent in size and scope to the meat section in our supermarkets—and includes all kinds of seafood from squid to prawns, mussels, oysters, crabs, lobsters and seaweed. Lamb and pork tend to be cheaper than beef since they're not so popular with the Japanese. Beef and chicken tend to be sold thinly sliced for use in stir-fry recipes or cooking in a pot. Beef tends to be expensive because it's mostly imported—'Aussie Beef' is quite popular.

- Fruit is seasonal. The most affordable fruits are bananas, oranges, *mikan* (small mandarins), kiwi fruit and strawberries.

Some different kinds of fruit you might want to try are *nashi* (a cross between an apple and a pear), *mikan* and 'melon'. 'Melon' look like rockmelons on the outside but are green on the inside like honeydew melons. They tend to be very expensive, up to ¥5000 for one which seems to justify the fact that they're sold in elaborate gift boxes.

- Vegetables tend to be reasonably priced, particularly if you try the ones popular in Japanese dishes, such as *daikon* (white radish), *gobo* (burdock—I'd never heard of it either) and *shiitake* mushrooms.

- Pre-cooked foods are readily available as most supermarkets have a kitchen out the back where they prepare all kinds of cheap, convenient foods such as *sushi*, steamed vegetables, *tempura* and grilled fish.

- Some supermarkets and department stores have a bakery on the premises, specialising in continental style bread, cakes and pastries. Otherwise you'll have to content yourself with the packaged stuff. Tip Top has nothing on these guys—loaves are sold in packs of six slices, with each slice about 3 cm thick, sweet and white. Larger cities also have French-style bakeries (one chain is called Train D'Or), health food shops and bakeries.

- The dairy section in supermarkets seem to be expanding as the Japanese develop a taste for dairy foods such as cheeses, yoghurt, milk (which tends to be quite watery), butter, margarine and ice-cream.

- Most supermarkets have several kinds of *tofu,* noodles, seaweed, sauces and dressings, as well as the standard items found in any Western supermarket. If you get peckish while shopping, there's always the free samples: cheeses, snacks, fruit and other delicious tidbits.

A typical shopping list (for a few days) would consist of fruit (bananas, kiwi fruit, plums, peaches) for about ¥2000; vegetables (carrots, broccoli, lettuce) for about ¥600; bread (six slices) for

¥180; spaghetti, ¥200; canned fruit, ¥200 and *tofu*, ¥80. An all up total of ¥2660.

The Foreign Buyers Club (FBC) is a mail-order company that was set up in 1987 by two Californians and has grown into a huge operation that can ship almost anything (mostly American products) anywhere in Japan. Although based in Kobe, most of their business runs from its mail order catalogues and website: www.fbcusa.com. You pay when you order, all staff speak English and delivery takes up to 30 days. The FBC has three divisions. The General Store offers more than 40,000 items from the US including medicines, personal care products, drinks and baby products. The Corner Store-Deli has specialty food items from all over the world, and American magazines. The Corner Store-Learning Centre offers more than '1000 of the best English teaching materials, books, children's videos, games and CD-ROMs.' For more information or a catalogue, call 078-658-0032 or go to www.fbcusa.com.

Health

Health insurance. In a country where people wear surgical masks over their mouth and nose when they have a cold to prevent spreading germs, and the average life expectancy is 80 years for women and 74 years for men, you'd expect health standards to be high. And they are. But hand-in-hand with good medical care come high medical costs, which is why it's a necessity to have health insurance, even for short stays. There are a few options:

- Travel insurance is good if you're staying for less than six months but it can become expensive if you're planning to stay longer. Also, many policies won't cover you when you are working or travelling to and from work.

- You can take out your own health cover. One popular (English-speaking) company that offers health insurance for foreigners is Global Health Care Ltd. Based in Auckland, New Zealand, they cover foreigners from any country living in any country *other than their own*. This is a good option if you're working full-time and your employer can't cover you; or if you're not working full-time; or if you're on a Working Holiday Visa. The best thing about this kind of insurance is that it covers you on your travels outside Japan too. Global Health Care's quarterly premium is USD$200 – 300 depending on your age and the kind of policy you sign up for. You'll have to pay your medical bills and then lodge a claim for reimbursement. For details call (64) 9377 5958.

- National Health Insurance is for those who are working full-time and whose employer will pay part of the premium (they'll usually pay 2/3 and you'll pay the rest). Not all employers can or want to subsidise employees' health care; it usually depends on the size of the company. To apply for National Health Insurance, take your Alien Card and passport to the city office and ask for the insurance counter ('*Kenko hokken no kakari wa doko desu ka*'). Once there, ask for national insurance cover ('*Hokken ni hairitai no desu ga*'). They'll give you a National Insurance Card which, like your Alien Card, you must carry with you at all times. If you need medical treatment for whatever reason, simply show your card and you'll only have to pay 30% of your medical bill. If you're caught without your card, you'll have to pay the full amount and then apply at the city office to be reimbursed with the difference. Note: working holiday visa holders can't apply for National Health Insurance.

Health care for *gaijin*

- There are some health risks to be aware of, even if you can't do much about them. The air quality (humidity mixed with pollution) in major cities can cause problems for people with respiratory problems such as asthma. Smoking is widespread (cigarettes only cost about ¥240 a pack) so it can be hard to avoid passive smoking. Eating raw fish (*sushi* and *sashimi*) and raw beef (*tataki*) pose no known health risks, although there are food poisoning scares in Japan as there are in any country. Only globefish (*fugu*) is known to be toxic and that's so expensive there's not much chance you could eat it unknowingly.

- Many hospitals (*byoin*) in Japan have English-speaking staff. The average stay for in-patients is much longer than in hospitals back home, which is one way that treatment can start becoming expensive. Also, people tend to go to hospital in Japan in the way we go to our GP back home. It's not because they're overreacting, that's just the way the health system is set up. Doctors (*isha*) actually supply the medication they prescribe to patients instead of sending them to a pharmacy, and it's been suggested that this has led some doctors to over-prescribe. To find an English-speaking doctor in your local area, check the English Telephone Directory, ask a friend or enquire at the Tourist Information Centre. When visiting a doctor or hospital you usually don't have to make an appointment, but you do have to pay on the spot. The *Berlitz* Phrasebook has a good section on seeing a doctor. In case of emergency, try memorising this phrase: '*Isha ni tsurete itte kudasai*' ('Please take me to a doctor').

- Dentists (*ha-isha*) are so expensive that people have been known to fly to Taiwan or Hong Kong for treatment and still save money. The Japanese tend not to be as concerned as Westerners about having straight teeth. It's rare to see children wearing braces and there's still debate in some areas over whether fluoride should be added to metropolitan water supplies. There was a time when protruding canine teeth were thought to look very appealing.

- Alternative health practices are increasing in popularity including: Chinese herbalism (*kampu*); acupuncture (*hari-kyu*); *reiki*; moxibustion (*o-kyu*); hot springs and mineral baths (*onsen*); and Shiatsu massage. Word-of-mouth recommendations will lead you to practitioners in your local area.

- Counselling services are available in most major cities with many operating 24 hours a day. Newcomers to Japan run into difficulties more often than most would admit. Even if you don't think your situation is bad enough to warrant counselling, it can help to have a chat with another *gaijin*, someone who understands the problems of living in Japan and how you might be feeling. For services in your area, consult your English Telephone Directory or the foreigners' magazines. Some are also listed in the Appendix.

A day in the life of a Tokyo alien

You wake up a bit before midday, depending on the amount of travel time between your apartment and your workplace, which can vary from 10 minutes to three hours. Usually I had to be at work about one in the afternoon. You go over to your refrigerator, it's pretty small and only comes up to your thighs. There's nothing in it of course, so you grab a piece of thick white toast and some coffee. Or you leave the house, after showering and getting into your work clothes, and go to Mister Donuts.

You trudge on down to the subway station. The subways are extremely clean and very punctual. If the schedule says the train will be there at 9.53, it will be there at 9.53. It will not be there at 9.52 nor will it be there at 9.54. You can definitely set your watch by it. You get on the train, sometimes they're very crowded, so you'll have to stand up for most of your ride. There's lots of different kinds of people: salarymen, high school students, old ladies, children. All kinds of people use the subway because it's an extremely effective form of transportation in Tokyo. It's really difficult to own a car—you have to pay for parking and the upkeep of a car in Tokyo is just astronomical—so it's not unusual for a very prosperous businessman in Tokyo to take the subway.

At one o'clock, it's not that crowded. But Tokyo's a city of 12 million people, so at any given time they all have to be somewhere. They even have a schedule for high schools where at certain times of the year some of the students are in school and some are not. Kind of a rotation shift because there are so many students and not enough classrooms.

You'll arrive at your place of work [usually an English school] with seconds to spare before your first class, and you'll teach English all day. You'll get a dinner break for about an hour during which you'll run out and try to find something cheap to eat. For the first three months I lived in Tokyo I had *gyudon* every day. *Gyudon* is a bowl of rice with grilled beef, onion and soy sauce on top. There was one place called Yoishinoya Gyudon, which is like the McDonalds of *gyudon* restaurants. It's something like ¥600 for one bowl.

So you eat that in seconds and then you go and have a bit of a wander around. The vibe in Tokyo is kind of stiff. It's not really vibrant or anything. It's got a very businesslike feel. It doesn't feel like Soho or Broadway where you walk through it and bounce along. There's nowhere in Tokyo like that. I think that's what I miss most being in Japan, the general feeling that you get from being in different areas of the city. Tokyo's just sprawling, you can get on a train and go in any direction for two or three hours and it still looks like Tokyo, still looks the same. But there is a certain excitement about it being foreign. I remember when I first got there, I got a sense of 'Wow! This is electric!' and it's a really Asian culture. Now there are a lot of foreigners in Tokyo but at any given moment you'll still be the only foreigner on the street, in a sea of black hair and brown eyes.

When the clock hits 9 pm [the end of your work day] you're brain dead. You've ad libbed so many of your English lessons. You're hungry and tired. So instead of going home you decide to go and have a drink. You might go down to the spot where everyone comes together, which is near some big TV monitor in the centre of town. There's places in every city where lots of foreigners pass by and meet each other.

You'll see some friends and they'll say 'Hey, there's a cool *izakaya* (Japanese pub) I heard about, let's check it out'. So you go to this *izakaya* and before you know it you've had four beers (each about ¥700-800). You've eaten a few plates of food, *sashimi*, some *champon* (noodles), some *gyoza*, some chicken wings. But you have to remember that you don't want to miss your last train, which is around midnight or 1 am. The last train is always packed because that's everyone's last chance to get home. If you miss that, it's an expensive taxi ride home or a sleepless night in a 24-hour *ramen* shop where you just eat *ramen* and sleep in the corner until the first train the next morning. Or if you've still got some cash left, you might go to a bar that stays open until 5 or 6 am. Then you take the first train home, get to sleep about 7 am and wake up a bit before midday. (By Peter Moses and Vince Panero).

Life as a rural alien

You wake up late, maybe 9.30 am (at least it feels late when all your neighbours are up and about by 6 am). The sun's already shining in your eyes through the clear top half of the sliding glass doors that open onto the outside mini-verandah. You roll up the *futon*, put it in the cupboard or just in the corner, to clear some living space. If it's a sunny day you might put it over the railing outside to air. Apartment blocks on clear sky days take on the multicolours of their *futons* over every balcony, clipped on with big plastic clips so they don't fall into the street and smother passers by below.

After breakfast—a cup of tea and a thick slice of white toast— you leave the house. You're getting used to putting your shoes on at the door, just as you're getting used to sleeping on the floor, eating with chopsticks at every meal, sitting down to have a shower, not locking the house when you go out and cruising the streets on your 50 cc scooter.

If you've got the day off, you might go to the beach. You ride your bike past the *obachans*, the old women working in the rice fields, dressed in neck-to-knee work clothes, big straw bonnets shading their smiling leathery faces. *Ohayo gozaimasu*! (Good morning!) you call out to each other. Stooped from too many years bent over, some of them look like they'll never straighten up again. You might have a swim or walk along the black sand, dodging the obstacle course of concrete typhoon barriers every 50 metres or so whilst beachcombing for shells or debris that's been washed ashore—once I saw an endless line of strawberries and cherry tomatoes littering the high tide mark. If the wind's blowing offshore, there'll be fishermen letting out floating kites, each one armed with fishing hooks and lures that dangle into the water. And on weekends, whole families come to wiggle their toes in the wet sand for pippies which they collect for their *miso* soup.

If it's a work day you'll get back home, shower, scoff your lunch (leftover rice out of the rice cooker with pre-cooked veges or fish) and leave the apartment by 12.30 pm whizzing into the city centre on your scooter. If you're teaching private students in their homes, it's like visiting friends all day: at each one there's a cup of tea or coffee and some cakes or snacks waiting for you (at this rate you won't need dinner). The students are fun and chatty, making the lessons pass quickly. Still, after a few hours of making up games or thinking of topics of conversation you feel drained, so you stop at a vending machine for a can of coffee. It's too hot to hold in your bare hands in winter but icy cold in summer, either way it's sweet and milky and gives you a good caffeine hit when you need it. An isotonic drink's marginally healthier, you might have a Pocari Sweat (where do they get these names?).

Your last lesson finishes around 9 pm and you get home around 9.30–10 pm. It doesn't feel late, this being the normal knocking-off time for English teachers in Japan. *Gaijin* often meet each other for dinner around this time. You operate on a different body clock setting than you would back home. Tonight you get a *bento* dinner on the way home: a takeaway box with chicken, rice and a token salad (your favourite is chicken *namban* for ¥430). The women at the *bento* shop know you, since you go in there at least three nights a week. They ask how you are and you feel that your Japanese has to be improving through these little encounters.

When at last you get home—shoes off at the door—you greet your *gaijin* flatmate. '*Tadaima*!' ('I'm home!') and she calls back from the kitchen, '*O-kaeri*' ('Welcome home!'). In winter your house is so cold it's not unusual to get home, have dinner and then drive to the local *onsen* (hot spring baths) which are open until 2 am. They're only 10 minutes away and you can soak in the soothing, therapeutic water for as long as you like. You return home feeling warm and relaxed all over, unroll your *futon,* slide the paper door to your bedroom closed, pull the cord on the overhead light. '*O-yasumi nasai*!' ('Good night') we call out to each other through the paper walls. *Ii yumei mite.*' ('Sweet dreams'). By the author.

Working

Japan offers the foreigner an extraordinary work environment. Even in these tougher economic times, it's one of the few countries in the world where you can work fewer hours than you would back home and earn higher hourly rates in a currency that's relatively strong. There's a big range of jobs but needless to say, the most popular involves some kind of English teaching.

Are there still jobs in Japan?

The 1980s are generally regarded, by *gaijin* at least, as the 'golden age' of working in Japan. It was a time when you could arrive in Japan armed with little more than the ability to speak English better than your students, land a job as a revered English teacher and within a few days be earning a ridiculous amount of yen for simply chatting to a few willing students.

Along with the economy, the job market tightened up through the 90s and with fewer jobs available, the work scene became more competitive. For English conversation schools you needed some qualifications: the minimum being TEFL or TESL diplomas and/ or a Bachelors degree. But jobs were still fairly thick on the ground for those with the right combination of skills, looks and luck.

What does all this mean if you're heading over to Japan now? The good news is that, at the time of writing, although Japan's economy is still sluggish, the Japanese, after a period of cutting back on luxuries such as English lessons, are starting to loosen up again. You only have to flip through *gaijin* magazines such as *Tokyo Time Out* to realise that there are still plenty of English teaching jobs on offer and, as Japan realises the increasing need, in the internet age, to communicate with the outside world, translators and interpreters.

It might take you a little longer to find work now than it would have ten years ago (the average time is now around two months, so it's a good idea to be financially prepared) but the poor performance of the Australian and New Zealand dollars recently has become a huge plus for antipodeans, at least, to work in Japan. Though payment rates haven't increased much in the last few years, today's exchange rates make working in Japan almost as lucrative as it ever was. For instance an average starting salary of ¥250,000 per month at an English conversation school is now equivalent to about AUD$4300 per month, whereas a few years ago it would have been worth half that amount. While the cost of food and entertainment has risen a little in Japan in recent years, your income is generally going to be generous enough to allow you to have fun and save some yen.

One thing remains the same: given fewer working hours than most jobs back home, working in Japan is still a lifestyle choice offering experiences not available elsewhere.

Visas and programs

There are several ways to work in Japan, the most common being the:

- work visa (usually obtained in Japan, although you can organise it before you go if you have a sponsor)
- JET (Japan Exchange Teaching) Program (you must apply in your home country)
- working holiday visa (you must apply before leaving home).

The work visa

Work visas are available to anyone of any nationality and vary according to the kind of work you want to do in Japan. They're valid for up to three years (it used to be only one year, but the three years is still at the discretion of the issuing authorities), depending on the category of visa you get and the contract with your employer. Depending on your nationality, there are between 10 and 15 categories of work visa: there are visas for professors, artists, engineers, journalists, business managers, accountants, medical personnel, researchers, entertainers, and (the one most foreigners go for) teachers.

Although you can apply for a work visa before you go to Japan, the usual procedure is to get there and find an employer who is willing to sponsor you. When you arrive in Japan you'll be issued a temporary visitors visa at the airport. This visa entitles nationals of Ireland, the UK and some other European countries to stay (without working) for up to six months; Canadians, Australians, New Zealanders and Americans can stay for up to 90 days. This gives you some idea of the time frame for finding a sponsor since the temporary visitors visa prohibits work of any description.

When you find an employer (say an English conversation school) who is willing to be your sponsor, ask them to contact the local immigration office and make an application on your behalf for a Certificate of Eligibility (issued by the Ministry of Justice in Japan). Once you have the Certificate of Eligibility, you have to front up at the nearest immigration office yourself. Take your passport; one passport-sized photograph; your Japanese sponsor's name, address and phone number; and two copies of your Certificate of Eligibility (the original and a photocopy). When you finally get your work visa (it might take a few weeks), you'll have to leave Japan and re-enter on your new work visa (since you're not allowed to work on your temporary visitors visa). Most *gaijin* just fly over to Korea for a few days to do this.

If you can line up work in Japan before you arrive (covered elsewhere in this chapter), you can apply for a work visa in your home country. Same procedure: ask your employer to obtain a Certificate of Eligibility and have them send it over to you. You must organise your visa and arrive in Japan within three months of the Certificate of Eligibility being issued otherwise it will expire and you'll have to go through the process of getting another one. It's worth noting that if you find work before you leave home, your new employer will often take care of all the visa protocol for you. This is true of the English conversation schools that have recruiting offices overseas.

If you need to leave Japan while you're on a work visa, you'll need to get a re-entry permit (multiple re-entry is best), which costs up to ¥10,000.

The JET Program

The Japan Exchange Teaching (or JET) Program was set up by the Japanese government in 1987. It's a cultural exchange program aimed at fostering better international relations between Japan and participating countries. The idea is to encourage young university graduates to go to Japan, share their experiences with Japanese high school students and, at the end of their two-year stay, return home with favourable impressions of Japan and the Japanese people, fostering better international relations between Japan and the rest of the world.

Every year, about 1500 new JETs are recruited from more than 37 countries including Australia, New Zealand, the US, Canada, Britain, Brazil, China, France, Germany, Ireland, Korea, Mexico, Peru, Portugal, the Russian Federation and Spain. There are currently more than 5800 JETs employed in Japan. The majority are from the US (about 2500), Britain (1100), Canada (900), Australia (400), New Zealand (300) and Ireland (100).

To become a JET (as they're called), you need a Bachelor's degree or need to be qualified to teach at primary/elementary schools, and be between 18 and 35 in July of the year you apply. You apply in your home country by getting an application form from your nearest Japanese embassy or consulate and if you're accepted your work visa is taken care of. The ads for the program usually appear in the press each December and you'll fly to Japan (all expenses paid) in the following July. Note: if you've already been a JET or if you've lived in Japan for three years or more since 1990, you are not eligible for the JET program.

There are three kinds of JETs:

1. Assistant Language Teachers (ALTs) who comprise 90% of all JETs. Each ALT is assigned to a junior or senior high school. To give you an idea of the scope of the program, every high school in Japan has either an ALT on staff or a visiting ALT (they visit a number of schools in their local area, each one at least once a week). ALTs don't need to be able to speak Japanese as you'll be expected to only conduct lessons in English.

2. Coordinators of International Relations (CIRs). These JETs usually have a working knowledge of Japanese (sufficient to work in a Japanese office) and are employed in nine-to-five administrative jobs in local government offices, on school education boards and at international centres. Their role is essentially to liaise between a community's local and foreign populations. Their duties include interpreting at international events, giving advice on planning and designing international exchange programs and entertaining overseas visitors.

3. Sports Exchange Advisers (SEAs). As the newest kind of JET (this category was created in 1994), SEAs usually have some background in physical education since their role is to promote international relations through sport. They usually work in prefectural offices and their day-to-day work includes coaching, training and planning sports-related events. Only a few SEA positions are made available each year.

As an ALT you're assigned to a high school somewhere in Japan, where you 'officially' work a 35-hour week. Because you're an assistant language teacher, you always teach with another teacher and may have little chance to plan your lessons or teach what you would like to teach. You're only expected to teach conversation (the Japanese teachers teach English grammar, reading and writing) so your hours of actual teaching time can be few and far between; however you're often still expected to be at the school for a full day, every day. You get weekends and public holidays off. Your contract is for one year, renewable in July each year with a maximum stay of three years. The Japanese government looks after its JETs: they subsidise your apartment, help you organise furniture and a car, and give you 20 days paid holiday per year—all in addition to your monthly salary of ¥300,000. They'll even help you find a job back home when you leave Japan.

Being a JET's really good. The first year is challenging, it's a new culture, with new rules, learning how to be a teacher. The second year you're learning how to do it properly. The down side is it's a full-time job and you're in the school situation full time so you have to learn how to deal with the

Japanese system. There's a lot of frustration, it's a very different culture as far as work goes. But as far as having so much free time, it's the opportunity of a lifetime. Some JETs become black belts in karate, study Japanese or write novels, you always leave with something. Dave MacKail, a Scottish law graduate, after his third year as an ALT.

The working holiday visa

The working holiday schemes are agreements between the governments of Japan and Australia (in 1980), New Zealand (in 1985), Canada (in 1986), France, Korea (both in 1999), Germany (in 2000) and the UK (in 2001). As of 2000 more than 42,000 working holiday visas had been issued since the program started. These agreements allow nationals of these countries to live and work in Japan, while at the same time allowing Japanese to live and work in the other countries. The aim of the programs, according to the Japan Association for Working Holiday Makers website, is to 'promote mutual understanding between our respective countries and to broaden the international outlook of our young people'.

You are only allowed one working holiday visa—so it's literally a once in a lifetime opportunity—regardless of whether you stay three months, six months or the maximum 12 months.

As a working holiday maker you have advantages compared to those with work visas. A working holiday visa frees you from the bind of an employer who is also your sponsor. You have the freedom to do freelance work for several employers at once or to move around, working in different parts of the country for a few months at a time. You can even choose how many hours you want to work each week.

To be eligible for a working holiday visa you must:

- Be an Australian, New Zealander, Canadian, French, South Korean, German or British citizen (and living in your home country at the time of application).

- Be between 18 and 25 (sometimes 30) when you apply.

- Have a valid passport and return travel ticket, or sufficient funds to purchase a return ticket.

- Have proof of reasonable funds to cover your living expenses until you find work (which can be up to two months). Unfortunately the immigration officials probably won't believe that you can live on US$10 a day so they insist on a minimum of US$2000 (US$3000 for a married couple) or equivalent in your national currency.

- Be in good health, with no criminal record.

- Intend to primarily holiday in Japan for a specific length of time.

To apply for a working holiday visa, allow at least three weeks before you intend to leave. You have to apply in person (your mum can't do it for you) and in your home country by visiting your nearest Japanese embassy or consulate (see Appendix for addresses and contact details). You can apply on the spot, but there's usually a bit of paperwork, so it's best to either pick up the working holiday information sheet or call and ask for one to be mailed to you. There's no fee.

Your application will consist of:

- Your passport which should be valid for the period of your stay.

- The application form (available from your nearest Japanese embassy or consulate) completed in duplicate.

- Two identical passport photos.

- Two copies of your resume/curriculum vitae (CV) or personal history, including educational background, work experience, hobbies and interests.

- Proof of a recent medical exam (Canadians only).

- A detailed itinerary. Remember, the Japanese government sees the working holiday as more 'holiday' than 'work' (literally 'an extended holiday while engaging in temporary employment in order to supplement your travel funds'). If you're like me, you won't have a clue what you'll be doing a week after you arrive, let alone six months after. Don't panic—you don't have to be too specific—just make sure you say that you'll be moving around the country quite a bit.

- A brief letter outlining your reasons for applying for a working holiday visa. It's a good idea to include things such as an interest in travelling around Japan, learning the language, learning about Japanese culture and visiting friends.

- Proof of adequate funds (a return air ticket, bank statement, travellers cheques, etc).

Your fresh working holiday stamp is a single entry visa valid for six months from the date of arrival in Japan. You must enter Japan within six months of the date of issue. When you get to Japan the immigration official at the airport will stamp your visa with a date. Take note of this date as if your life depends on it because, in a way, it does: overstaying your visa is a serious offence. Every year at least 1000 illegal aliens are deported (though they tend to be mostly other Asians working illegally).

The rules of the working holiday visa

- You can work part-time or full-time as long as your stay is 'deemed to be primarily a holiday in Japan.' The main restriction, according to the Ministry of Foreign Affairs, is that you're not allowed to work in places that are regulated by the long-winded Law on Control and Improvement of Amusement and Entertainment Businesses, which means nightclubs, bars and gambling establishments such as Pachinko parlours.

- Jobs should not be sponsored, i.e. you're not allowed to contract to an employer to work for a year at a time. You're also not supposed to organise employment in Japan before you arrive.

- You are required to pay 20% income tax which is automatically deducted from your monthly pay cheque.

- The working holiday visa is a 'single entry' visa which means that it entitles you to enter Japan *once*. If you want to leave and re-enter Japan while your visa is still valid, you'll have to get either a single re-entry permit for ¥6000 or a multiple re-entry permit for around ¥10,000 from your nearest Immigration Bureau. If you don't do this, your visa will be automatically

cancelled as soon as you leave Japan, even if you're only away for a few days.
- The visa is valid for an initial stay of six months, after which you may be able to extend it for another six months (at the discretion of the immigration authorities). You can only extend your visa once. Australians are however, able to extent it twice for a period of 18 months.

Extending your visa is an exacting process. Before your first six months are up (i.e. before the exact date stamped on your passport), you'll have to decide if you want to stay in Japan for up to six months more, or if you're ready to leave. If you want to stay, you'll have to visit an immigration office and ask them to extend your working holiday visa. It's a good idea to call the immigration office before you go (or ask a Japanese-speaking friend to call for you) to check when it will be open. In country areas one immigration official often has to service several offices so they might only be at each office one or two days a week. Take your passport, Alien Registration Card and at least ¥10,000 to cover the renewal fee (about ¥5000) and any other costs such as stamp duty, extra photos or a re-entry permit (if you're planning to leave Japan and re-enter before the next expiry date). Keep in mind that no visa renewal is automatic, even if you've been working and holidaying by the rules, but there are a few things you can do to help your cause: dress conservatively, be polite and humble, and whatever you do, don't let on that you speak any Japanese—the more you know, the more questions they'll ask.

Where to start

Working websites. There's a plethora of websites to help you look for work whether you're in Japan already or yet to leave home. Here are a few to get you started:

JET Program: www.mofa.go.jp/j_info/visit/jet/index.html

Everything you need to know about the Japan Exchange Teaching Program including how many JETs go every year, types of positions, how to apply and testimonials.

Jobs in Japan: www.jobsinjapan.com/ Assists foreigners find work in Japan. Listings for teaching, IT, bilingual positions, modelling, acting and agency jobs. You can also post your resume for free on the noticeboard.

Tokyo Classifieds: www.tokyoclassified.com A weekly e-zine with jobs listed by occupation from accounting to travel. Includes articles about people who work in Japan, problems and new opportunities.

Overseasjobs: www.overseasjobs.com Worldwide job listings that you can search by location or job type e.g. 'teaching English'.

Japan Unlimited: www.japanunlimited.com Living, working and travelling in Japan. Classifieds, embassies, business hours, public holidays, useful phone numbers and FAQs about working in Japan.

Gaijin Pot: www.gaijinpot.com A groovy website offering services to job seekers and employers with database of jobs and tips for job seekers. Search for jobs online or receive emailed listings.

Japan Interactive Guide: www.japanig.com General info about working in Japan, visas and working holidays.

Work in Japan: www.workinjapan.com/wij/ Specialises in technology and media jobs; you can create your own resume.

See the Appendix for the website addresses of the Japanese embassies which include lots of information and useful links to other relevant websites. Alternatively go to your favourite search engine and type in appropriate key words.

Other beginnings. This will depend on where home is. If you are from a country that has a working holiday agreement with Japan (Australia, New Zealand, Canada, France, South Korea, Germany, the UK) then you can apply for a working holiday visa or the JET Program (provided you meet the various criteria) or seek an employer to sponsor you for a work visa. This may be necessary if your age prevents you from applying for the working holiday visa. If you are from a country without a working holiday agreement with Japan then you can apply for the JET Program or seek an employer to sponsor you for a work visa.

Because Australia has had a working holiday agreement with Japan longer than any other country (since 1980), there are two organisations in Australia that have, over a number of years, been able to connect many working holiday makers to a job in the hospitality industry. Hospitality Japan and World Education Program have arrangements with Japanese employers seeking English speaking staff for hotels, resorts and on the ski fields. Both of these organisations are able to accept applications from those holding a working holiday visa regardless of the country they come from. See page 139 for more details.

For Canadians, SWAP (Student Work Abroad Program) runs a program for those eligible for a working holiday visa. This program consists of a pack of services including accommodation for the first two nights, an orientation in Tokyo, a mail drop and other services. It does not link you up with a job but Canadians with a working holiday visa are however, eligible to apply for job contacts through Japan Hospitality and World Education Program mentioned above. For full details about SWAP contact a Travel CUTS office, a list of which can be found at www.travelcuts.com. Otherwise go directly to the SWAP website at www.swap.ca.

If you would like an English conversation school to sponsor you, there are four schools with recruitment offices outside Japan: Nova, GEOS, AEON and Shane. Nova (at www.teachinjapan.com) has offices in Australia, New Zealand, the UK, Canada and the US. GEOS (at www.teaching-english-in-japan.com) has offices in the UK and Canada. AEON (at www.aeonet.com) has offices in Australia and the US while Shane (at www.saxoncourt.com) has offices in the UK. You'll need to meet the minimum educational and experience requirements for these schools to consider your application. You may however prefer a job other than English teaching. This will require searching different avenues, some guidelines for which can be found in this book.

If you travel to Japan to seek employer sponsorship then your trip will be tinged with some uncertainty about the cost of finding a job. However as explained in this chapter this task is not insurmountable but you must have enough money to support yourself for say, two months. And, as outlined in the Living chapter, there are many ways to cut the cost of living in Japan.

Teaching English

It's hard to envisage a time when teaching English won't be the job of choice for foreigners in Japan—it's been that way for so long now, and for good reason. It's one of the few jobs in the world that allows you to work minimal hours for more money than most of us could earn back home in a regular day job, and often the only qualification required is that you're a native English speaker. Because most classes consist of conversation practice, you don't need to be a teacher or have any teaching experience. You don't even need to be able to speak Japanese.

Time and money are perhaps the most attractive aspects of English teaching. As a guideline, you start work sometime in the afternoon (usually 1 pm) and teach into the evening (about 9 pm): the after-school and after-work hours will be your busiest times of the day. Even working 4 pm to 9 pm five days a week, which is reasonably common, you can easily earn enough to live on. Work longer hours in a city teaching job, maybe supplemented with a little private tutoring, and your earnings can go into orbit. The most common scenario is to work 40 hours a week (10 am to 7 pm Monday to Friday) and earn ¥250,000 per month with subsidised accommodation and transport to and from work. When it's converted back to, say, Australian dollars (AUD$4300 per month) it's a generous salary in anybody's language.

You don't need to speak Japanese to teach English in Japan. It's not as unlikely as it sounds. Even looking for teaching work isn't a problem since English schools are one of the few places where you're guaranteed to find at least someone who speaks English, even if it's just another teacher. As for the teaching itself, Japanese is rarely spoken in the classroom so you'll often find yourself in the bizarre situation of being in a foreign country and working in your native language. You don't even have to explain English words or phrases in Japanese: most of your students will have studied English at school for six years, so they'll usually be able to understand you if you speak slowly enough and clearly enough for their level of ability. With a textbook, a few props (pictures, tapes, videos, newspapers, etc) and your trusty English–Japanese dictionary for back-up, you won't have any trouble communicating. Besides, most of your students expect (and are paying for) as much exposure to English as possible, even if it means struggling to understand what's being said.

You don't need any teaching qualifications. Times have changed since the first plane load of *gaijin* descended on the teaching scene and found that if they spoke more English than their students they had a job. In recent years, many smaller conversation schools have been going out of business, resulting in fewer teaching positions and more competition. The minimum requirement for most teaching jobs is now a Bachelor's degree (or equivalent) in any subject. If you have any technical qualifications you'll be able to broaden your student base by finding highly paid work teaching groups of, say, doctors or engineers on their company premises.

You don't need any formal teaching qualifications to teach English in Japan, but a diploma or certificate in TESL/TEFL (Teaching English as a Second/Foreign Language) or TESOL (Teaching English to Speakers of Other Languages) can give you an edge if you're after the top jobs in Osaka or Tokyo.

You don't need any teaching experience. It may sound strange, but you don't need to be a teacher to teach English in Japan. This is partly due to the fact that many employers (particularly large conversation schools) put you through their own training. Most also have detailed syllabuses and textbooks to follow (removing the need for you to do your own lesson plans). Due to the strict nature of Japanese high schools and Japanese society in general, discipline is rarely a problem (particularly as most of your students or their parents have paid handsomely to have you teach them). But the real reason why most English teachers in Japan don't need to be qualified teachers is that the post-school English learning process is geared almost completely towards teaching students how to speak and listen to spoken English.

Learning any language, of course, involves some conversation practice but in Japan this is particularly true. They're not called 'conversation schools' for nothing. The reason for this is that most Japanese undergo six years of exam-oriented English lessons and by the time they leave school, they can barely speak a word. They're 'false beginners' in that they might sound like beginners when they're trying to speak, but their vocabulary and knowledge of grammatical rules are usually excellent. So they need practice listening and speaking with real, live native English speakers. 'Free conversation' is the official term for when your whole lesson involves talking about what everyone did on the weekend or discussing the latest movie. You might play word games like Scrabble or UNO, read an English language newspaper or learn the words to a new English pop song. In fact much of the time you won't feel like a teacher at all, and more like the token *gaijin* who's there to speak and show how to pronounce things 'correctly'.

So what DO you need to be a successful English teacher? You need the ability to encourage your students, enough patience to wait for them to agonise over how to answer even the simplest questions, compassion and an understanding of their difficulties. You'll soon notice differences between Japanese adolescents and those 15 to 16 year olds you know back home. Though generalisations are often little more than stereotypes, it's worth being prepared for the fact that your Japanese students may be shy, unassertive and afraid of making mistakes. At such times, the most effective thing you can do is provide an accepting environment in which they can safely make mistakes and thereby learn. They'll also expect you, as the teacher, to take the lead, start the conversational ball rolling, structure the lessons a little and tell them what to talk about next. Above all, don't take it too seriously and you'll go far—a sense of fun has saved many an English lesson!

Deciding what kind of teaching job you want

There are lots of ways to teach English in Japan. The options include: teaching in an English conversation school (*eikaiwa*) or at a *juku* (a cram school), private English teaching, and one-off teaching positions at international schools, universities and junior colleges, even an organic farm! These are explained below, but as you're reading it's worth thinking about what you'd ideally like to get out of teaching English. Do you want to experience working with kids? Perhaps your main aim is to make as much money as you can, or have as much free time as you can to travel and pursue other interests. Do you want to work in a big school with multiple benefits or a smaller school with more flexibility? Do you want to gain experience teaching a foreign language? Or maybe you just want to see if teaching is the profession for you.

English conversation schools

You'll travel to work out of peak times, usually by public transport, bicycle or scooter so you leave home around 12.30 pm and leave work in the evening around 9 pm. You'll be working in an air-conditioned office environment, probably with other teachers (so even though you're on your own for each class, you'll have some moral support at other times). You might have to help out with some office work when you're not teaching or preparing classes. You'll either teach regular hours (1 pm to 9 pm or 4 pm to 9 pm are standard) which means regular pay (an average salary for 25 hours of class time per week is ¥250,000 per month). Or you'll just come in for the hours you teach and be paid per lesson (usually about ¥2000 to 2500 per lesson, but it depends on the school's location, size, number of students, etc). You'll be teaching in a classroom but the size of classes varies from a handful (or even one-to-one) up to 30 students. Lessons are usually 50 minutes with 10 minutes preparation time (or a breather) between classes. Some schools don't have breaks between classes, but they might have longer breaks mid-afternoon when there are no students booked in. Usually there's no take-home work like marking (tests are rare and any homework you give will be checked in class) and barely any preparation. Once you get the hang of it, it'll only take a glance at the relevant chapter in the textbook to prepare for your next class.

There are more than 8000 English conversation schools in Japan. Every major urban centre has at least one, most have several, and big cities have hundreds. So the odds are in your favour. There are various types of schools, from small independent ones to large national schools that have a branch in every major city.

Small schools tend to recruit locally and irregularly—usually when one of their teachers is leaving—so you have to keep your ear to the ground to find out about openings. The main advantage of working at a small school is the flexibility. They often can't afford to sponsor many (if any) teachers, or they might not have enough work to fulfil the requirements of those needing a full-time position for their work visa. So they're well suited to working holiday makers who can arrive, start work immediately and stay for a few months.

The down side is that getting a job at a small school usually requires some legwork. You'll have to find out from another *gaijin* the names of all the schools in your area, then start calling or sending your CV (it's usually better to call first to find out if they are even interested in employing any new teachers). When you call, tell them your nationality and your visa status. And if a school offers you a few hours a week, take it (at least if there aren't any other options on the horizon): when they see how you handle the teaching game, they might reward you with more classes; it'll give you the chance to meet other teachers who might know of teaching jobs in other schools, or private students who want lessons and you'll find your hours increasing in no time; at the very least you'll gain first-hand experience of teaching in Japan.

Larger national schools such as Nova, GEOS and AEON generally require a longer term commitment than the smaller ones. Most of their teachers are on sponsored work visas (not working holiday visas) so there will tend to be a greater mix of nationalities, many of whom have been recruited overseas. Those schools without overseas recruitment offices generally send interviewers around the world to interview candidates for the coming teaching year. Bear in mind that the Japanese academic year starts in April. You'll often see ads in your home newspapers (such as *The Sydney Morning Herald*) as well as in the English newspapers in Japan (the most well-known is *The Japan Times* on Mondays).

There are advantages in working at large schools: they often have schools all over Japan; you can apply for work in your home country and be set up when you arrive; they might help you organise your visa; some schools arrange affordable (even subsidised) furnished accommodation for you (usually an apartment); they can get you discounts on airfares and meet you at the airport; and most offer orientation sessions on arrival covering such topics as alien registration and coping with a new culture as well as aspects of your new job.

The benefits can often be better at larger schools. The starting salary at Nova, for example, is ¥250,000 per month (¥259,000 in Tokyo) and this increases after your initial two months to around ¥265,000 to 289,000 (depending on where you're working). They also offer two weeks paid annual leave in your first contract plus a week off over New Year and pay for your transport to and from work. Applications are accepted year round and one-year renewable contracts begin every month except December.

The working conditions at larger schools tend to be more structured than at smaller schools. You're usually required to teach at least 25 hours per week, with starting times varying throughout the week (e.g. you might start at 10 am on Mondays, have Tuesdays and Wednesdays off, and start at 1 pm the other days). It's common to have your 'weekend' during the week, and to work at least one day on the weekend. As a native English speaker you'll be teaching advanced students (the beginners' classes are taught by the school's Japanese teachers). Sometimes there are strict rules regarding socialising with your students. Some schools even have video cameras set up in the classrooms to ensure that teachers don't stray from the curriculum.

It's worth noting that some schools (big and small) practise a subtle form of 'discrimination' in relation to their preference for teachers. Many prefer their teachers to speak American English, in line with most of the teaching materials used (such as textbooks, videos and audio tapes). If you have a broad Australian or Scottish accent for example, you might have more trouble finding work than if you have a more neutral accent. However, there is a growing acknowledgement that English is a language of many forms and increasingly schools hire to reflect that diversity. There's also some reluctance to hire non-native English speakers (i.e. people whose first language isn't English) but this happens more in rural areas than in big cities.

Sometimes there's a preference for female teachers, largely because the majority of students are female and they feel more comfortable learning from a female. On a more serious note, some schools have been known to reject applicants, even native English speakers, if they don't look like 'native English speakers'. The preferred look is Anglo-Saxon, i.e. fair hair, blue eyes and fair skin. If you don't fit the preferred description, stick to the bigger cities where diversity is more accepted.

When it comes to the interview, remember that a cheerful personality and a cooperative and patient attitude will pave your way to finding a teaching job sooner than qualifications and teaching experience will. Remember too that most English conversation schools aren't run by teaching professionals or educators. They're often run by business people and entrepreneurs. How you present to them (in all ways) shows them how you'll present to the students, so make sure you dress conservatively and neatly.

Things to check before you take the job

- Teaching conditions. Ask about the number of students per class and how long each class lasts. The standard length is 50 minutes, while kids' classes are from 45 to 50 minutes and adults' classes can be up to two hours. How many hours per week are required in various duties, including face-to-face teaching, preparation and office work? Are you required to stay at the school between classes? Can you take time off and how much notice do you have to give? How many other teachers are there? More teachers means more moral support and help in preparing lessons and getting into the swing of things, and if you're sick or want a day off you might be able to swap shifts.

- Are there any specific school rules? Some schools don't allow teachers to 'fraternise' with the students. This is usually based on the fear that you might try to take the students away from the school, or at least become friends with them so they get to practise their English for free and so no longer have a need for lessons.

- Teaching materials. Does the school provide them? Can you use your own materials sometimes? Is there a set syllabus to get through? Some schools promise their students coverage of a certain number of chapters or proficiency tests after they reach a certain stage in their lessons.

- Pay. Will you be paid per lesson (many smaller schools pay this way) or given a monthly salary (which could mean when you're not teaching you might be expected to hang around in the office)? Are there any employee bonuses or extras like travel costs? When is pay day? (A general rule is 25th of each month and most schools pay monthly in arrears.) How will you be paid—cash in hand or direct to your bank account? Does your pay automatically increase after you've worked there for a certain time (usually a year)? Cancellation pay: do you still get paid if your students don't show up? Are there many compulsory social outings? (Most schools have teacher–student parties for Japanese occasions such as cherry blossom viewing, and non-Japanese occasions such as Halloween and Christmas.)
- Is there any training? Is it in-house or will you have to travel? (If you're not in Tokyo or Osaka they might fly you to another city.) Training can seem an attractive bonus and a confidence-booster when you've never taught before, but bear in mind that the classes are generally conversation classes anyway. If all else fails you can just talk to your students until you get the hang of teaching. Also check if you still get paid during training (you might not want to put off getting that first pay cheque).

Juku

A *juku* is a place where school students can take extra lessons in specific subjects, including English. Most school students (not just those who are lagging in their studies) go to a local *juku* at least two nights a week. If you work at a *juku* your hours are usually from 6 pm to 9 pm, teaching a classroom of 20 kids, although often the class will be broken down into smaller tutorial groups. As with conversation schools, you'll mainly be teaching English conversation, perhaps with some 'team teaching' where you work with a Japanese teacher and demonstrate how to pronounce words correctly. You might be required to teach at different places on different days, in which case you'll need transport.

Finding *juku* is generally a little more tricky than finding English conversation schools. They tend not to be listed in the English

Telephone Directory or other directories. The best way to find out about this kind of work is to ask other *gaijin* or ask at the English school where you'll be working during the day (lots of teachers supplement their income in this way and some English schools even run *juku* in addition to their regular classes, often at a different location). Rates of pay have dropped since the boom times of the 1980s and range from ¥2000 to ¥5000 per hour. Some *juku* offer salaried positions, which can involve teaching three hours per day (6 pm to 9 pm) five days per week for, say, ¥170,000 per month.

Private English teaching

Private English teaching offers the most flexibility of any English teaching job but it does take some time to establish yourself. This isn't as hard as it sounds, however. Most foreigners, even those with full-time teaching jobs, find that after a month or two of teaching they find a steady stream of people who either want to learn English themselves, or know someone who does.

As a private teacher you have a price advantage: even if you're charging standard rates it's still far less than students would be paying at a school. One national English conversation school, for example, requires students to pay monthly fees of ¥10,000 in advance for four lessons (one per week); another school charges ¥15,000 per person per month for twice weekly lessons; both were for group lessons. By way of comparison, I taught a class of three high school girls in their home, and they each paid ¥5000 a month for four one-hour lessons (so my total payment was ¥15,000 per month). Students usually pay cash (handed to you in an envelope) monthly in advance.

Private English lessons are also more personal—the students can have the teacher all to themselves, often in their own home, so it's convenient, there's less embarrassment about making mistakes in front of other students and there's more chance of the students learning what they want to learn.

At first, the idea of teaching privately might seem a little daunting. You have more freedom to make up lessons and you don't have to follow a school syllabus, but with this comes more responsibility. So if you've never taught before it's a good idea to get some teaching experience in a conversation school before launching yourself into the private teaching scene. This also gives you some 'street cred' in the eyes of your students and with this can come the ability to charge what you think you deserve. It also helps to wait until you have a little knowledge of Japanese, even basic greetings (which only takes a month or so) so that you can negotiate lesson times and rates with your students.

One advantage of working at a school is that you get to use all their teaching materials including cassettes, textbooks, games and the TV. When you're on your own, you have to get your own materials together, which can include:

- A textbook. Check with your students first as they might have one they like. For many students, particularly high school kids who spend so much of their 'free time' studying, they won't want to use a textbook at all. In this case they'll generally say they want 'conversation practise', which means talking about whatever they are interested in (you might want to brush up on the latest Japanese pop stars and bands in this case!).

- Conversation-prompting material. There are times, even with the most fluent students, when you'll need props to help the conversation flow and provide some kind of framework on which to hang the day's talking. If you're thinking about making 'privates' your main source of income in Japan, it's worth thinking about getting some teaching materials before you leave. Or once you're in Japan, the Foreign Buyers Club has more than 1000 English teaching aids, available by mail order or through their website at www.fbcusa.com.

You'll also have to find your own students. You might inherit them from a fellow *gaijin* who's leaving or your Japanese friends might have friends who need lessons. Make it a habit to give your business card to any new Japanese person you meet—make sure it says 'English teacher/tutor' and has your contact number. You could even put up a notice at your local community hall or try printing up a flier saying you're looking for students and stating your experience, any relevant credentials and your contact details, but don't be surprised if this doesn't work too well, since the Japanese are reluctant to deal with people they don't know. Just don't, whatever you do, try to lure students away from the conversation school where you teach (or even from other schools). It's severely frowned upon, and can only hurt you in the long run since word spreads quickly around the English teaching scene.

Working out what to charge for private lessons can be tricky. If you do take over classes from another *gaijin* your new students will generally be happy to pay what they were paying their former teacher. But for new students you'll have to decide what to charge. This will depend on several factors:

- Location. The going rate is higher in major cities where students potentially have more disposable income than in country areas.

- The distance you have to travel to get to class. If you teach them at their home you can probably charge a bit more, and they'll probably be willing to pay a little more for the convenience of studying in their own home. I had one student, a well-to-do housewife, who paid ¥4000 for each one and a half hour private lesson in her own home, i.e. ¥16,000 per month (which was what her former teacher charged).

- How many students are in the class. More students require more preparation so you can be justified in charging more (by the hour) if you're teaching three people than if you were teaching one, but it should still be cheaper per student the rate for a one-to-one lesson.

- The length of the lessons. Kids can cope with 45 to 50 minutes, high school students with one to one and a half hours, and adults, with up to two hours.

- The time of the class. Since you'll be more in demand for evening and weekend classes, you can charge a bit more for lessons at these times; for daytime classes, which are less popular, you might have to settle for a lower fee.

- Who your students are. Doctors, dentists, airline pilots and entertainers will often pay more for English conversation

(¥10,000 per hour is not unheard of). To get to these students you'll have to target them. The best way is to give your business card out to any professionals you happen to meet socially. In some cases you may need to know appropriate professional jargon but you can sort that out beforehand.

- Ask other foreigners in your area what they charge. As an example, you might charge up to ¥8000 per lesson in Tokyo. But in a rural area you're more likely to charge ¥5000 per person per month for weekly lessons, with say three or four students.

A few basic teaching tips will help you get started. As a general rule, try to make lessons fun and interesting. Otherwise young kids will get bored and besides, high school students seem to have so little pure fun in their lives. I wish I had ¥100 for every time I've asked a high school student what they did on the weekend and they answered, 'I studied' or 'I slept' (to catch up on all the sleep they missed by studying so hard during the week!). Often it's not even their choice to study English with you (it's their parents' choice), so they might bring a negative attitude to the class to start with (along the lines of 'English has never been fun before, with all that grammar and study at school, so why should it be fun now?'). I used to think of my classes as a bit of a mission—if only to keep myself interested week-in and week-out—not so much to teach them something, but to give them a little relief from all their hard work and something to look forward to each week.

Always allow your students time to warm up. They might not have spoken a word of English since your last lesson. Ask them what they've been up to since you last met, let them talk as much as they want to, or ask them direct questions to get them thinking.

Make up a few stock dialogue situations (such as eating in a restaurant, shopping, asking directions, reporting a crime to the police, planning a holiday or going on a quiz show) or get your students to make up their own scripts.

Ask your students to prepare a talk about something. Suggest a few topics such as 'My Best Holiday', 'My Job', 'My Classmates',

'What is Sumo?', 'A Funny Thing That Happened to Me' and so on. Or ask them to bring a photo or object from home and talk about it.

Games are a great way to loosen things up. If you end every lesson on a happy note (with a game or something that's fun for them), your students will always look forward to the next lesson. Kids games include UNO (a card game), probably the most played game in English classes in Japan since it's good for any level (even preschoolers can use it to learn about colours and numbers). You can get them to draw pictures from English commands, e.g. 'draw a red flower'; a more advanced version of this is to give one student a picture and get them to describe it to another student who has to draw it.

There are plenty of word games for older students. For example, 'Who Am I?' where one student thinks of a famous person and the rest of the students take turns asking yes or no questions to find out who the person is. There are countless variations such as, 'What Am I?', 'What's my Job?' and 'Where do I live?'. How many questions can you ask your partner in 30 seconds? Make a story with everyone in the class adding one sentence. You can even bring along a board game such as Scrabble or Monopoly.

There's an almost infinite number of games you can adapt to English learning. There are language camps around the world that teach kids a sport such as skiing or surfing, in a foreign language. You can use that principle in your classes too. Remember you have almost total freedom when teaching privately. You might want to take your kids to the zoo, the local park, a festival (get them to explain to you in English what's going on!) or the beach. Chances are they'll be happy to hang out with a *gaijin* for a couple of hours anyway. For adult students you'll often find they'll invite you out for dinner, on day-trips to the mountains or somewhere you never would have gone on your own.

Just keep in mind, in all your dealings with private students, that what most of them want out of an English lesson is not just an opportunity to practise hearing and speaking English, they want a bit of fun too!

English teaching on a commune

Teach English on an organic farm and live as part of a commune in Hokkaido, within yodelling distance of some of the finest mountain scenery in Japan. It's not as far-fetched as it sounds. The *Shin Shizen Juku* (New Nature School) is not the only commune to offer English teaching positions in Japan but it is the only one that accepts *gaijin*, usually working holiday makers, on a casual basis.

Shin Shizen Juku has been operating for 20 years from a small organic vegetable farm in the village of Tsurui-Mura in north-eastern Hokkaido. The commune makes its living by growing vegetables and teaching English in neighbouring villages and towns, and employs foreigners as 'volunteers' to help on the farm and teach English for 10 to 15 hours per week (hours are dependent on how many teachers there are at any one time). The income from teaching is used by the commune to pay for electricity, oil for heating (it gets down to $-20°C$ in winter!), food, visits to the *onsen* (hot spring pools) and a party once a month. In exchange for teaching you receive expenses (petrol, bento money), all your meals and accommodation. You might be required to help out in the vegetable garden or cut wood for the wood stove, but you'll have lots of free time to go hiking, fishing and cycling.

I've been here for two months and it's pretty good, it's a pretty chilled out place, really rural and you can get into the community stuff really easily— I had a chance to do some [traditional Japanese] *taiko drumming. It's more about English teaching than farm work. And it's a great place for side trips: within an hour there's lots of* onsen, *lakes and mountains.* Sarah Cowell, an Aussie working at the commune for a few months.

Shin Shizen Juku prefers volunteers to stay for three to five months to give some stability to the English lessons and the life of the commune. For those who want to stay six months, there are extra benefits: an allowance of ¥50,000 to 70,000 per month and free Japanese lessons (six hours each week). If you want to visit the commune for a few days without working, room and board costs ¥2000 per day. Contact Mr Hiroshi Mine, *Shin Shizen Juku* (New Nature School), Tsurui-Mura, Akan Gun, Hokkaido 085-12. Tel: (0154) 64 2821.

One-off teaching positions

International schools are generally located in areas where there's a sizeable foreign community, usually American and British expatriates working in Japanese or foreign companies. Students at these schools are either children of these expats or children of well-to-do Japanese parents who want to give their kids a head start in the English-speaking world. The most prestigious institution is the American School in Japan in Tokyo. Teaching at an international school can be a good option for qualified teachers wanting to gain some teaching experience in addition to the experience of living in a foreign culture.

Universities and junior colleges. Teaching at a university can be frustrating work: once students pass the entrance exam (which has basically been the ultimate goal of their entire school lives), they tend to relax. As they see it, they've spent the better part of their youth studying their brains out and now it's time to kick back. Besides, if they're enrolled at a good university, they're virtually guaranteed a job when they leave regardless of whether or not they study. A junior college is more like a technical or community college or a polytechnic with two-year courses that focus on specific jobs, so the students tend to be a bit more conscientious.

Teaching at junior colleges and universities can be lucrative (teachers can earn up to ¥8500 per hour) but jobs are hard to come by. To get a foot in the door you need to have been in the teaching scene in Japan (preferably in high schools) for at least a couple of years to have built up a reputation and contacts. Or you'll have been employed at a university or technical college outside Japan. There are few positions available, currently only about 150 *gaijin* are teaching full-time at Japan's 1000 or so universities and junior colleges.

How to find English teaching work

Word-of-mouth. As soon as you arrive, even if you're not ready to work, put the word around that you're looking for a teaching job. Even friends who seem to have no connections whatsoever can hear of a *gaijin* who's leaving their job in a few weeks, or they might have a Japanese friend who's going overseas and wants to take a crash course in English before they go.

The internet. Apart from the websites mentioned earlier in this chapter, the following two deal specifically with teaching jobs.

ELT News: www.eltnews.com/eltnews.shtml News about the English teaching scene in Japan, articles, interviews, company profiles, ideas and activities for the classroom and detailed job listings.

O-Hayo Sensei ('Good morning, teacher'): www.ohayosensei.com An informative fortnightly newsletter about teaching in Japan. Includes detailed job listings, info about teaching materials, online articles and accommodation classifieds.

Let's Japan!: www.geocities.com/lets_japan/index.htm is an irreverent look at English teaching through the eyes of those who do it—the teachers themselves. Also lists a few 'approved' schools. The name is a play on the name of a well-known conversation school called Let's English.

Cold call all the English conversation schools in your area. You'll need to get hold of a list of the schools: check the English Telephone Directory for your city, ask other *gaijin*, or enquire at the nearest international centre or JAWHM. Maybe some of the schools themselves will even help you (if they don't have any positions available they might suggest other schools to try).

English language media. *The Japan Times* has employment classifieds on Mondays and *The Daily Yomiuri* has its classifieds on Wednesdays. Then there's *Kansai Time Out, Kansai Flea Market* (Kansai is the region around Osaka) and *Tokyo Time Out*, which all come out monthly, and *Tokyo Notice Board* which is weekly.

'ENGLISH TEACHER wanted for children. Native speaker only. Sign-up bonus ¥50,000 for new teacher. Kitty Club in southwest Tokyo. 03-5702-1615.' *The Japan Times*

'ECC NAGOYA seeks full-time English Teachers (29.5 hr wk), teaching kids and adults. BA required. Visa sponsorship and training given. Travel and relocation assistance may be available. Start dates in March and April. Contact the Personnel Dept. at (052) 332-6156, fax (052) 332-6140. E-mail: ecchr@spice.or.jp' *The Daily Yomiuri*

'Seeking native speaker for informal English conversation group. Itami City, one day per week (flexible). ¥6,000/hr. Please call 090-8230-3158.' *Kansai Time Out*

'FULL-TIME ENGLISH TEACHERS WANTED. Temporary positions for correspondence and telephone teaching available starting at the beginning of November, ending approx. the end of February. All work done in the office. Gross pay ¥13,000 per day: Mon. to Fri. 9am to 5pm. Average monthly salary approx. ¥270,000 plus transport allowance. Dependent on satisfactory service, a bonus of ¥50,000 paid on completion of the contract. Must have appropriate visa. Please send resume by fax to: 03-3363-8546.' *The Japan Times*

'A part-time British instructor wanted for courses in British English. Proper visa is essential and must live in Osaka-city. Pay ¥3,000 plus transportation up to ¥500. Call Osaka School of English. 06-6608-4133. Mon.-Sat.10:00-18:00.' *Kansai Time Out*

'SHIZUOKA UNIVERSITY. Full-time English teacher. Native speaker. 58 or older. Japanese ability. Begins April 1, 2001. Contact (054) 238-4288/4291 or ektsira@ipc.shizuoka.ac.jp' *The Japan Times*

'F/T, TT ENGLISH teacher wanted! Experience in teaching a must. 25hr/week, ¥320,000 a month. Please send resume to MERRY ENGLISH CLUB Fax: 0794-33-2277.' *Kansai Time Out*

'EXPERIENCED English instructors for corporate classes needed in Osaka/Kyoto/Shiga/Nara. 1. Full-time (native) 2. Part-time (native/Japanese). Call CTS 06-6229-2123.' *The Japan Times*

The best times to look for teaching work are September and March. The academic year begins in the first week of April. Full-time teaching contracts usually start and finish in March—although many large English conversation schools recruit and place English teachers in schools year-round. For casual teaching work, try applying before the summer holidays (mid–July to mid–August): during the break conversation schools will still be open but their full-time teachers may want to escape for a holiday. Schools are likely to be closed for up to a week in early May (Golden Week) and New Year (around 27 December to 3 January).

Non-teaching jobs

English teaching might be the most popular job for *gaijin* but it doesn't suit everyone. Which is not a problem since there are lucrative, fun and, challenging jobs for the willing *gaijin* all over Japan. Many of these jobs are called '*arbeit*' (derived from the German word for 'work') which means 'part-time work.' With all the advantages of English teaching jobs, you might be wondering why anyone would bother doing anything else. Two returned *gaijin* tell why they took the road less travelled.

This [life in clubs and bars] is the real Japan. In English teaching, your students want to be like you, like a Westerner, but in the clubs they tell you jokes, they're rude to you. You think they're really shy people, but they're not. You think they're innocent, but they're not. I thought they were family orientated, but they're not in the slightest. I knew guys that didn't even know how old their kids were. The order is: job, friends, then family. Tammy Smith, an Australian who worked as a hostess in Osaka.

My aim was to keep away from teaching jobs and maximise my time speaking Japanese. English teaching was what all the foreigners did, I wanted to do something different. Jess Halford, an Australian who worked in a factory and a car wash.

The following will give you some idea of the kinds of non-teaching jobs available. Though there are lots of other opportunities, finding them is half the fun.

Hostessing

Japan's hostesses have a bad name overseas, particularly with reports of foreign women being mistreated (or worse) at the hands of their employers. This is definitely one area where it pays to be extra careful in deciding who you work for. That said, it can also be an interesting and (if you work for a ethical employer) safe experience that offers unique insights into Japanese society and financial rewards unmatched by most other jobs in Japan.

Hostesses are basically the modern day *geishas* of Japan. Originally, *geisha* meant 'talented person', one who could sing, dance, act and play music, and essentially this is now the role of the hostess. *Geisha* clubs still exist, but they're priced beyond the reach of all but the most generous business expense accounts, so most businessmen go to hostess bars instead.

A hostess bar is like an ordinary bar but with a number of women (typically 10 to 15 hostesses) whose job it is to wait on tables and entertain and flirt with the men who visit. And that's all. One important thing to understand about hostessing is that it's not equivalent to being an escort or prostitute. There's no pressure to grant sexual favours (prostitution has officially been illegal in Japan since the 1950s) and it's even been said that the women in hostess bars are incidental anyway, just part of the equation that allows the menfolk to relate to each other for business and political purposes. That said, however, certain elements of society still regard hostessing work as 'improper' and hostesses can receive negative vibes from people in Japan as well as back home. To be on the safe side, it's often better to say you work in a bar or club than to say you're a hostess.

You usually work from 6 pm to midnight, or 8 pm to 1 am or 2 am every night. In one year of working I had only four days off, but work was fun anyway, and you have your days free. You sleep til 3 pm, then you get up and get ready. You definitely have to look the part, which means full make-up, your hair done, you have to wear a skirt or dress, the shorter the better. I was recruited with three Australian friends, and we were all taken shopping [in Sydney] and allowed to spend AUD$2000 each on designer clothes, anything we wanted. Stockings are compulsory, shiny ones, preferably. Pants are not allowed. And in some clubs the hostesses are even required to wear a 'uniform' of a bikini or swimsuit, even a playboy bunny outfit.

So you get to the club around 6 pm or 8 pm. Your duties vary according to what kind of club it is and how high class it is. In the smaller clubs, where it's just the mama *(female club owner) and the* shacho *(the boss), the hostesses have to help with everything. At my first club I had to do general cleaning, sweep the floor, set up the karaoke machine, get the ice containers ready and roll the* oshibori *(hot hand towels the men use to wipe their hands before eating or drinking). At bigger clubs you can just show up when your shift starts.*

Then you have to greet the customers, take them to a table. For new customers, the shacho *might pick three or four girls and say, 'You, you and you, go over to that table'. If it's busy usually four men will get four girls, eight men will get six girls. And for that night and any subsequent nights they come back, they are your customers. Some top managers of large corporations might come to the bar three times a week, just to relieve the pressure of their jobs. Young guys come too, usually with the older guys. You'll usually have a couple of tables to attend to, that's maybe six or seven people to entertain in a night, all at the same time.*

In Japanese society women are a little lower in status than men, and that's how the hostessing job works. You have to do little things for them. A good hostess will wipe the condensation off her customer's glass, fill their glasses, escort them to the karaoke stand and maybe even sing a duet with them (if you can sing you'll win big tips, and the more Japanese songs you know the better the tips), applaud them, feed them their food (usually just snacks), peel their grapes (really), get them their hot towels and dance with them. You get propositioned at least once a night but you've just got to make a joke out of it. Say you've got plans so they won't get offended and you can keep them as customers. A good hostess 'takes it on the chin'. Most of the guys are happy just to have you sit with them anyway, you're like an accessory.

There are 'penalties' for things like yawning in front of the customers. Or if you're not dressed properly and fully made up, with your hair done, you might be sent back to your apartment, or you might have to sit at the bar all night, which severely limits your earnings since you can't pick up any tips. But gaijin *hostesses get more chances than Japanese hostesses simply because they give the club status. That's why you're hired in the first place, for your image.*

At the end of the night, the customers tip you directly, in cash (up to ¥4000 per table) and you see them out. They might ask you out to dinner or out on a date, or on to another club. If you go on a date, you usually have to ask your boss for permission and give details about when you'll be back. I always took my two friends along, you just ask the customer if you can and usually it's the more the merrier and they don't mind. When you get a new customer you get his business card and you keep it, you're supposed to ring your customers after they've been, to say you miss them and ask when they're coming to the bar again.

It's a bloody hard job: really draining. You've got to keep the conversation going, you've got to put up with people who've been sick in the toilet, who are chain smoking, grabbing you, and then you've got to sing! On the plus side, you can see a lot of things in Japan for free. I've been to Disneyland, to Mt Fuji. You can go to all the clubs, meet heaps of people. You can learn Japanese really quickly. You can even get English teaching jobs! Tammy Smith, who used to work as a hostess in Osaka.

The minimum hourly rate for hostess work is ¥2000, so if you work five hours a night six nights a week, you can earn a minimum of ¥60,000 a week. Sometimes all your expenses (like your apartment, gas, electricity and a food allowance) are paid by your employer—about ¥10,000 per week. Free drinks while you work is standard. A good deal is ¥3000 per hour (with tips on top of that) plus accommodation.

What you need for the job

- Only females are employed in hostess bars, but there are 'host bars' where all the staff are male.

- This is the original 'mingle and smile' job. You need to have reasonable looks but it's more important to be able to chat about anything that comes up in a light, breezy manner. The men who come to hostess bars as a rule don't want intelligent conversation from you, you're there to provide moral support and to laugh at their jokes. There are literally thousands of hostess bars in the Tokyo Ginza area alone so there's a lot of competition for customers. If you keep your customers and bring in new ones you'll be very popular with the boss. This may allow you to negotiate for better pay.

- You don't need any experience, and you don't need to be able to speak Japanese. In fact sometimes the men prefer it if you can't understand them. It's been suggested that they get a feeling of superiority from keeping you in the dark about what they're saying. Plus, in the larger cities the businessmen often want to practise their English. Of course if you do speak Japanese you have an advantage, particularly in terms of being able to negotiate your conditions of employment; and it'll be more fun if you're able to talk to the Japanese hostesses and bar staff.

- It helps to be a good drinker and to like spirits (most Japanese businessmen prefer scotch over beer). Not only does it make some of your customers more bearable, but it keeps your boss happy since the more you drink, the more your customers drink, and the more money the bar makes. An average bill for a table of two guys who have the services of two hostesses can be around ¥20,000 and some customers chalk up bills of up to ¥100,000 in just a few hours. They have to pay a cover charge, table charge, an ice and water charge, as well as for food, drinks and *karaoke*, and a hostess charge (per hostess generally for a two hour period and extra after that).

- A level head. You can't trust everyone you meet in this industry, and you don't get something for nothing. As Tammy says, 'Your customers tell you you're beautiful all the time and they might offer you things but they'll always want something in return.' The most successful hostess (in terms of earnings) is highly organised: she might write down the names of regular clients in an address book and call them at work to say how much she misses them and is looking forward to seeing them again at the bar soon. It's all part of the business.

- A sense of humour. If you can't handle people touching your hair, holding your hand or perhaps grabbing you as you walk past, you'd better stay away from this kind of work. In Tokyo there are bars where the hostesses are separated from the customers by the bar, but generally you're 'out there' with the clients.

How to find a hostessing job

- The English magazines (*Kansai Time Out*, *Kansai Flea Market*, *Tokyo Time Out* and *Tokyo Notice Board*) often advertise for hostesses but the ads aren't as common as teaching ads. Always make sure you check out any job offers before committing. Dodgy establishments still exist and it's not unheard of for places to make you work for a month and then not pay you. Some make you sign a contract, or keep your air ticket and passport as insurance that you'll stay with them. Others restrict your movements outside the bar (even during your free time). It's a good idea to work in a bar where there are other foreign hostesses, although sometimes they might not want you as competition. Some sample advertisements:

'Foreign girls wanted for work in friendly atmosphere in lounge in Sakai. Japanese ability preferred but not essential. Close to Sakai Higashi station. 8 pm-1 am. ¥2000/hour. Call (0722) 24 6734' *Kansai Time Out*

'Diamond Clubs seeking women for hostess/dancer position at various places. Terms and conditions are negotiable. Apt. provided. Call 090-4917-0340.' *Tokyo Notice Board*

'Club Vogue looking for hostesses. British, North Americans, Australian and German. ¥2000 to ¥4000 per hour, plus bonus. Mon. to Fri. Pay twice a month. Call after 8pm. 03-5563-7344.' *Tokyo Notice Board*

- Occasionally, hostess bars will advertise outside Japan. Tammy found her job through an ad in *The Sydney Morning Herald* that offered positions 'working in a hotel' in Japan. Make sure you carefully check what kind of work you'll be doing; it's easy to have false expectations and some employers take advantage of that. It can also help to apply with a friend (Tammy applied with three other Aussie girls she knew).

- If you're already in Japan, it's a good idea to visit clubs in person, but again go with a friend (say, another *gaijin* looking for a hostessing job). For some clubs you need to be introduced by someone who already works there, so ask around amongst other women you know.

- If you start working at one club you will often be approached by owners of other clubs who want you to work at their clubs, so you can get a better deal if you're not happy with the first place. It's generally not possible to work at more than one club at a time: it's a loyalty thing and anyway the sheer number of hours you're required to work at any one club tends to rule out that option.

Hosting

Host bars are the equivalent of hostess bars, except the tables are turned, so to speak. The staff are all male, the clientele all female, in fact many of the clients are hostesses who've just knocked off work. Because of the long hours they work, and the constraints it puts on their social lives, hostesses need somewhere to go and have a good time not unlike what they've been giving the men at their bars. As for hostessing, your duties as a host include sitting at a table with a few of the bar's patrons, talking, pouring their drinks, lighting their cigarettes and changing their ashtrays. As one host explains, 'The whole idea is to sweet talk, to schmooze, the customers, so they come back to request you. You have to really sell yourself.'

The pay is generally less for hosts than for hostesses—hosts get around ¥1000 per hour—but the work can become lucrative if you receive tips and presents from your clients. The main problem with host work is the limited market. There are fewer host bars than hostess bars to start with, and there's not the same demand for foreign 'hosts' as there is in the hostess scene.

It might seem like the ideal job if you like getting drunk and partying but there's a lot to put up with. You've got to be able to handle the long hours: working from 9 pm until 4 am or 6 am, because you're catering to the hostesses coming off work around that time. And long weeks, like you have to work six or seven days a week because you have to be there in case your clients come in and request you. You have to work in a smoke-filled environment, drinking with the customers every night, you can't just say, when it's time for another round, 'Oh, I'll just have a glass of water thanks'. And then we had to do a male revue, a 40-minute show three times a night. There's five or six acts in each show, and they vary from guys wearing special outfits or doing choreographed routines, but they all involve a finale of stripping down to a G-string. It's not on a stage, just in a cleared space between the tables. The 'girls' [customers] get quite carried away, but it's pretty low-key stuff. You're not selling your soul, it's not immoral or anything, it's just a form of entertainment. An Australian guy who worked in a Tokyo host bar.

What you need for the job

- You need to be able to speak a little Japanese (or a lot of Japanese if you want to work in a bar in one of Japan's smaller cities).

- You need to be well-groomed and well-dressed. Wearing a good suit, or else colourful clothes, can enhance your image amongst the patrons.

- You need to be polite and patient with your clients.

- It helps to have 'exotic' looks since host bars often like to have a range of 'looks'. 'In the bar where I worked there was one guy who was really muscly, a black guy, a kind of Latin-looking guy, and me, the tall guy. Only foreigners worked there,' says the Aussie host.

How to find a hosting job

To find a job as a host, word-of-mouth advice is the best way: just ask around in the foreign community.

Bar work

What's good about working in a bar is that you have more chance to improve your Japanese. Your days are free to roam around. You get free drinks and all the crackers you can eat! But you also have to remember that the Japanese have a different outlook on service. The customer is always right. And people tend to get away with a lot more when they're drunk. You have to remember not to take it personally if someone throws their money at you or barks a drink order at you, because that's just the way it is. The person serving is a non-entity, just someone who brings the drinks.
Peter Moses

There are several kinds of bars, from small ones that barely seat 10 people to large beer-halls. There are foreigners' pubs with names like 'Pig and Whistle,' although not all bars with English names are foreigners' bars. There are also the less familiar kinds of bars such as hostess bars and 'snacks'. A 'snack' is a small bar with hostesses, *karaoke* and a 'keep bottle' system (you buy a bottle of your favourite spirits, they write your name on it and keep it there for you, and when you come in you pay a table charge and order drinks from your own bottle).

Duties of bar staff are comparable to those back home, i.e. tending the bar and pouring and mixing drinks. Beer tends to be the drink of choice among Japanese, spirits among *gaijin*. Hours and rates of pay vary. You can work 6 pm to 1 am, 8 pm to midnight or 10 pm to 5 am. The more popular the club or bar and the later it stays open, the higher the pay. Rates start at about ¥800 to ¥1500 per hour; in Tokyo the hourly rate can be anywhere between ¥1000 and ¥2500, depending on the bar. Tips are rare, so your pay depends on your hours.

What you need for the job

- You need to speak at least some Japanese to work in a bar, unless you get a job in one whose clients are almost exclusively *gaijin*. In Tokyo you're more likely to find bars where only English is spoken, and you might even find a bar where another language is dominant. There are German bars, for example, where all the staff are German.

- Experience. Although it depends on the bar, how busy it gets and who the patrons are, the more experience you have the more likely you are to find work and receive higher pay. It might be a good idea to do a short bar course before you go to Japan; and remember to take any certificates, diplomas or references with you as proof of your experience and achievements back home.

- Most bar staff are male, for the simple reason that females wanting to work in this environment generally check out the higher paying hostess jobs.

How to find bar work

- Ask around. The usual way to find a bar job is by personally checking out all the bars in your local area, particularly the ones where *gaijin* hang out (this is a good option if your Japanese isn't so good) and just ask if they need any more staff.

- If your Japanese is good enough you can look around for pubs that have signs up saying 'Help Wanted' (in Japanese).
- Check out the classifieds in the *gaijin* magazines, for instance:

'The Shamrock Irish pub in Shinjuku is hiring waiters, waitresses. European or Australian preferred. Proper visa and Japanese ability required. Working hours: 5 pm—2 am. Please call for interview. 03-3348-4609.' *Tokyo Notice Board.*

'Hostess and bartender. North American with Japanese ability. Duties include entertaining by speaking English to our customers. Proper visa required. Orange House in Sasazuka. Call (03) 3378-2176 in Japanese after 8 pm or see www.sasazuka.net ' *The Japan Times*

'Part-time (from 2 to 3 days/week) foreign counter staff needed for hostess bar in Sakai. From ¥1500/hr between 20:00 and 01:00. Call Mr Nakamura in Japanese. 0722-22-2877.' *Kansai Time Out.*

Modelling

It wasn't long ago that Westerners in Japan were greatly sought after for their good looks and 'sex appeal' and if you were tall and foreign-looking you were virtually guaranteed a lucrative modelling contract as soon as you stepped off the plane. That was when Japanese models had a 'cute' rather than 'sexy' look and when the Japanese had an inferiority complex in the face of anything Western. But times have changed in the modelling world. For a start, Japanese models have become less cutesy and more worldly and are recognised as being at least as beautiful as their foreign counterparts.

The modelling scene in Japan is now dominated by professional models, both Japanese and *gaijin*, and Tokyo has become the highest paying city in the world. And as in any country, billboards and TV screens are plastered with the faces of supermodels and big-name foreign celebrities like Brad Pitt, Leo Di Caprio and Catherine Zeta Jones-Douglas, so that's who you're up against.

What you need for the job

- A professional attitude. Modelling is a serious business anywhere in the world, and particularly so with the top dollars (or yen) paid in Japan.

- Some kind of modelling qualification. It's a good idea to do a modelling course before arriving in Japan. Have a copy of your qualifications to show prospective employers.

- Some experience (anything is better than nothing) just to show you've worked before.

- A portfolio of professional photos. To get an idea of popular 'looks' in Japan check out a recent issue of one of the Japanese fashion magazines such as *Lee*, *With*, *Olive* and *Nonno* or the Japanese versions of magazines such as *Marie Claire*, *Elle*, *Cosmopolitan* and *Vogue*. Remember that as a *gaijin* you'll be expected to have certain attributes that Japanese models tend not to have, like light-coloured hair, blue or green eyes and long legs.

How to find a modelling job

- The most professional way to go about looking for modelling work is to register with a professional modelling agent before you leave home and ask them to line up a few contacts in Japan for you. As for anything in Japan, if you know someone you have a foot in the door.

- The English Telephone Directory lists modelling agencies in most cities. You can try 'cold calling' to arrange a meeting so that you can show them your portfolio.

- As soon as you arrive, set yourself up with a mobile phone so that you have a contact number to give out.

- The English language press advertises modelling positions fairly regularly.

    'MODELS. Experienced and inexperienced ¥30,000/day or more. For catalogs, special events, sales promotions, etc. Please send picture to TAKEO, Endless, Room 313, 1-30, 2-chome, Esaka-cho, Suita, Osaka 564-0063.' *Kansai Time Out*

MODELS (women & men) for photo and fashion wanted! Now free listing! Contact: 090-1586-6024; Email: 101237.3156@compuserve.com' *Kansai Time Out*

- Employment listings on the internet. The following ad appeared on the Tokyo Classifieds website (www.tokyoclassified.com):

'R&A Promotions is looking for foreigners for TV extras, CM and other promotion-type work. All ages and nationalities welcome. The famous TV star Thane Camus is with us. Just call 03-3225-3574 and catch your Japanese dream.'

Events work and acting

'Events' work involves being an announcer at department store launches of new products and demonstrations, and can pay about ¥30,000 – ¥50,000 a day. Following is a typical advertisement.

'BLOSSOM CO., LTD is seeking good natured foreign language speaking EVENT STAFF to register. Experience not necessary. Will discuss salary and conditions. Your resume needs to be sent by fax: Miyuki Aga (ms.) 06-6375-2308, include your nationality, height and your contact number.' *Kansai Time Out*

Acting is very competitive, and best left to the *gaijin* who've been living in Japan for years and have the scene sussed, at least until you get your own connections happening. That is, unless you see an advertisement like this from a talent agency:

'Wanted actors, models, voice actors + actresses any nationality to register for job openings. Please send your resume and photo to Meg. Fax 03-5376-2459, Tel 090-1420-2761. Email: Megmiaow@aol.com' *Tokyo Notice Board*

Jobs in the hospitality industry

Tourism is big business in Japan and getting bigger, with the average person's leisure time increasing (most Japanese workers now have both Saturdays and Sundays off!). Hotels and resorts are often so competitive that they apply strict criteria when recruiting employees and use overseas agencies to screen out unsuitable applicants. As a result, most jobs in the hospitality industry have to be organised before you go to Japan.

For most resort work, all you really need is a basic grasp of Japanese since your employer generally provides on-the-job training. Starting wages are in the order of ¥800 per hour. You're provided with free accommodation and all meals for the duration of your stay. Resorts jobs include waiting in resort restaurants, receptionist, concierge, bell person, housekeeper, kitchen hand, assisting guests with various sports and fun activities, and public relations. Qualified chefs are also placed at top resorts and hotels earning very attractive salaries. Large hotels might require you to do one job, such as receptionist or porter; smaller hotels could require you to do various tasks including working at reception, customer service, cleaning, preparing rooms and waiting on tables.

There are two agencies, both based in Australia, that handle these kinds of jobs: Hospitality Japan and World Education Program (WEP).

Hospitality Japan, based on the NSW central coast, specialises in finding work for young Australians, New Zealanders, Canadians and British in Japan's hospitality industry. Positions are generally for six to 12 months at well known hotels and resorts throughout Japan though most are close to Tokyo, with 85% of positions for waitstaff (waiters/waitresses). Placements are made with the intention of giving working holiday makers as much free/travel time as possible but an average salary is around AUD$500 per week. No previous experience in the industry is required, but it is essential to have some ability with the Japanese language, as well as 'the desire to travel, work and have a good time.' You also need to have your working holiday visa organised before applying (though they can help with your visa application).

Hospitality Japan's Working Holiday Placement costs AUD$950 which includes arranging free or subsidised meals and accommodation for the duration of your work contract; a confirmed work contract for at least six months (four months in the case of ski resort jobs); accompaniment to your hotel/resort from Tokyo; bank account and cash card (provided within the first month); and an English-speaking contact in Japan for backup support. Additional costs are for hotel accommodation and an orientation seminar in Tokyo on arrival (¥40,000), economy airfare to Tokyo (about AUD$1600 from Australia) and transfers from the airport (about AUD$60). For further details about Hospitality Japan programs, departure dates and costs, visit their website: www.hospitalityjapan.com.au or write to 2 Hillside Road, Avoca Beach NSW 2251, Australia,

World Education Program (WEP) has programs that are open to Australians, New Zealanders, Canadians and on British working holiday visas in Japan. WEP currently offers two programs: the Japan Ski Working Holiday Program and the Japan Hospitality Training Program. The ski working holiday program involves four months work in the Japanese ski fields, usually from December to April. Jobs include waiting in coffee shops and restaurants, portering, being a ski lift attendant or kitchen hand, checking lift passes and working in ski rental shops. The ski resort that employs you will usually decide what kind of work you'll be doing, largely based on your Japanese language ability. You can't choose which resort you'd like to go to, that's up to the resort's management, but at least you'll be in the company of other foreigners as the program is based around a group departure. Some small, family-run resorts might have only two *gaijin*, while major five-star resorts can have up to forty.

The Japan Ski Working Holiday Program costs AUD$3990 which includes an orientation seminar in Tokyo, meals and accommodation, a return air fare to Tokyo, transfers from Tokyo to the ski resort where you'll be working, and accommodation and meals at the ski resort. You're paid an hourly wage for working eight hours a day, six days a week. WEP has a Tokyo-based representative.

WEP's Japan Hospitality Training Program offers six to 12 months working in the hospitality industry. This program also costs AUD$3990 and covers everything the ski program does, as well as an orientation in Tokyo and information on living and working in Japan.

Applications for both programs are accepted year-round. There are no prerequisites as such; you just have to meet the conditions of the working holiday visa. You don't have to speak Japanese, although they do recommend that you take a short course in Japanese before you go, and your ability with the language will determine to some extent what kind of job you get. For more info contact World Education Program:

- In Australia: Level 12, 447 Kent Street, Sydney NSW 2000, Australia. Tel: (02) 9267 8755 or 1800 802 552 (from outside Sydney). Fax. (02) 9264 8135. E-mail: info@wep.com.au.

- In New Zealand: PO Box 31-762, Milford, Auckland, New Zealand. Tel: 09 410 8527. Fax: 09 449 2527. E-mail: wdarcy@wep.co.nz.

- In Canada and the UK: Email: info@wep.com.au.

Translating and interpreting

This is one job where, as in English teaching, being a native English speaker is a huge advantage thanks to the fact that Japan remains largely under-confident about its English language ability. Translating usually involves written material whereas interpreting involves the spoken word. The simplest kind of work in this area, and one for which you don't need to be a qualified linguist, is rewriting, i.e. converting a rough draft from something resembling English (also called 'Japlish' as it's like a language of its own) into readable English. Most translating work involves rewriting technical manuals (so some technical expertise can be an advantage); editing legal contracts, manuals and documents; and helping Japanese companies with their foreign correspondence. It's worth noting that just about every multinational corporation in the world has an office in Tokyo.

For those with strong writing and/or journalism skills and little knowledge of Japanese, there are also occasional jobs proofreading English documents that have already been rewritten (i.e. translated from Japanese), and transcribing tapes from spoken to written English (ready for translation).

Most translators and interpreters work freelance, either from home or their client's office. Full-time jobs are generally hard to come by—they usually involve being hired as an in-house translator and doing secretarial work when your translation skills aren't required. Rates of pay vary depending on your experience, Japanese language proficiency, and whether you're translating Japanese to English (as most English-speaking translators do) or English to Japanese, with simultaneous translators being at the top of the heap. Experienced simultaneous interpreters can earn up to ¥40,000 per half day although the starting rate is around ¥16,000 per half day.

Generally, though, you're paid not by the hour (or half day) but by the number of words you translate (for Japanese to English, it's the number of English words you produce), say ¥3000–3500 per 200 English words. To put it in perspective: an inexperienced translator may not earn as much as a full-time English teacher on ¥250,000 per month, but a skilful simultaneous interpreter could earn as much as ¥500,000 in the busy season (March–May and September–November). Bear in mind that translating and interpreting work is seasonal so it can be difficult to get a steady income just from this kind of work.

What you need for the job

- A high level of proficiency in Japanese including spoken Japanese, reading comprehension and writing ability. This means you should be able to pass the Ikkyu 1st rank, the highest level Japanese proficiency exam. Some specialised expertise is a definite advantage. According to a former interpreter, there's currently a glut of English speaking people in Japan, particularly in Tokyo: 'There are so many bilinguals it's really competitive, it's definitely more competitive now than it was 10 years ago. So you have to be really good, and be able to deal with a lot of specialised areas—medical, scientific, computer-related—not just the basic daily conversation. And because the bubble economy is no longer and the recession has caused companies to cut back, foreigners aren't leaving jobs like they did, so you don't see as many openings as before.'

- A knowledge of other languages can be advantageous—especially French, German and Spanish—for those Japanese companies that require help with sending communications to Europe.

How to find translating and interpreting work

- Register with an agent. Most companies deal with 'interpreter and translator agents' so to work in either of these areas it's a good idea to register with one, who then passes the work on to you. When you register, you usually have to do a test—your result on the test will determine your payment rate from then on.

- Check *The Japan Times* employment section on Mondays or place an ad in their classifieds, and the foreigners' press.

  'ENGLISH PROOFREADERS wanted. Native English speakers with adequate academic backgrounds (preferably PhD or master) in medical, chemical, computer-related or other fields. Call 0724-81-2061 between 09:00-17:00 (Monday through Friday).' *Kansai Time Out*

  'REWRITERS for leading science communications company. Excellent writing skills and appropriate scientific background required. All technical fields, especially semiconductors, mechanics, medical and bioscience. Work by email, fax, or take-home. In-house P/T positions also available. Fax resume with cover letter stating intent to Ms. Matsunaga, Forte, Inc., (03) 3354-9730.' *The Daily Yomiuri*

  'WANTED. 1) Experienced native English translators who are confident at writing well-phrased and natural sentences on general topics of translation. Also, translators with technical backgrounds for scientific or technical translation. 2) English native speakers to transcribe tapes in which English speeches from international symposiums, lectures, etc. are recorded. Japanese speaking ability not required. 3) English native proofreaders to check and brush up documents translated into English, who live in the vicinity of Kyoto. Fax or send resume by email to: Fax: 075-813-4050, or office@kiko-int.com Kiko International Co., Ltd. (www.kiko-intl.com).' *Kansai Time Out*

- Sometimes Japanese companies hire teachers from the big English conversation schools to do their proofreading and translating work.

Professional jobs

Whilst we're on the subject of professional jobs, it might be worth considering whether you can and want to look for work in other areas of expertise. According to *The Japan Times* employment classifieds, there are all sorts of opportunities in Japan for foreign web designers, accountants, bilingual secretaries, architects, public relations consultants, engineers, sales managers, etc. Most of these positions require some ability in Japanese, and experience. But they can offer real insight into the Japanese business world with all its customs, which might serve you well when you return home.

How to find professional jobs

- *The Japan Times* on Mondays is your best starting point, just to see what jobs are available. There are also websites listing professional positions as mentioned earlier in this chapter.

'ARCHITECTURAL OFFICE seeks experienced ARCHITECT. Requires Chinese (Mandarin) speaking/writing skills and good knowledge of Mini Cad/Vector Works. Please send your resume to SIA by fax, 03-3221-6510.' *The Japan Times*

'SAORA INC., an Indian owned Internet appliances and services company (see www.saora.co.jp) is looking for C++, JAVA, HTML PROGRAMMERS, SYSTEMS ENGINEERS, PROJECT MANAGER, MARKETING EXECUTIVE, SALES and ADMINISTRATIVE STAFF. Bilingual ability preferred but not necessary. Salary commensurate with capability and experience. Visa sponsorship available. Interested candidates of any nationality should apply by email or fax to personnel@saora.co.jp or (045) 913-9821.' *The Japan Times*

- For citizens from European Union (EU) countries, another option is the Executive Training Program (ETP), an 18 month program for young executives which the European Commission has been running for 20 years. The idea behind it is to train EU executives to enable their companies to become more effective in exporting goods and services to Japan and Japanese companies, thereby reducing the current trade imbalance between the EU and Japan. ETP applicants must be citizens of an EU country, have a university degree or equivalent, at least two years professional experience, and be employed by a company committed to doing business with Japan.

    The program runs over 18 months: the first 12 months involve an intensive Japanese language course as well as 30 lectures and seven industrial visits to Japanese companies. This is followed by a practical six month placement in one or two Japanese companies.

    Program organisers begin looking for candidates across the 15 EU countries in March/April and close applications by mid-September. They generally choose 40 to 50 participants from around 90 applicants each year. The successful candidates will depart for Japan in May. Note: both you and your employer must agree to participate—although there are lots of candidates who want to go, your employer needs to be willing to release you for 18 months and contribute to your living expenses in Japan.

    The cost of the program is split between the European Commission—who pays 120,000 euro (about £72,000) per participant to cover tuition, a relocation allowance and a monthly living allowance—and the participant's employer (who also pays transport costs to and from Europe). For more details visit the ETP website: www.etp.org.

- You could also try voluntary work to get your foot in the door, particularly if you're not desperate to start earning yen. When Jayne Fuller, a British lawyer, moved to Tokyo with her husband (who had just been transferred there for his work) her 'dependent' or spouse visa allowed her to work 20 hours per week. She approached a law firm she'd heard about from a friend in London, offered to work for free and soon found herself on a fully fledged work visa with full-time paid work (*Overseas Jobs Express,* October 15, 2000).

Now for something completely different: odd jobs

There are countless opportunities in Japan to work in areas outside the traditional *gaijin* occupations mentioned above, ranging between the extremes of conventional office work in a Japanese company to outlandish jobs you might never consider doing back home. They might not pay as well as teaching or hostessing, but they can offer varied experiences. To get some idea of what's out there, check out these advertisements (most from *Kansai Time Out*):

'Wanted full/part-time FOREIGN PROTESTANT CHRISTIAN STAFF as PASTORAL ASSISTANT, who helps conduct the wedding ceremony on Sats./Suns. ¥15,000 per wedding ceremony. Send your resume and the colour photo of you to the following address by mail. CHAPEL WEDDING MINISTRIES 1-1-15 Tanigawa, Daito-shi 574-0074. FAX. 072-870-5473.' *Kansai Time Out*

'GUEST SPEAKERS WANTED. Senri English Salon has weekly English conversation class on Wed. (18:30-20:30) near Senri-Chuo stn. Foreigners from any nation who can talk about their country, experiences, etc are welcome. We offer ¥5,000/class. Call Fumiko:090-9717-1898.' *Kansai Time Out*

'FM COCOLO is looking for a native English DJ for live programming. American, Canadian, or British preferred. Availability on Wednesday required. Contact Ms. Kaino via email: kumiko@cocolo.co.jp' *Kansai Time Out*

'Rollerbladers WANTED. ZESPRI, kiwifruits marketing company is seeking rollerbladers who can work for us in weekends this summer. Candidates must be over 18 years old. For details, email to: yoshimm.kiwi.co.nz' *Kansai Time Out*

'Kyoto fashion importer seeks full-time employee. Required: fluent English/Japanese, excellent communication, organizational, and computer skills. Preferred: fashion business and sales experience. Another World Co. Ltd. (Curtis or Miki). Tel: 075-241-0642. Fax: 075-241-1033.' *Kansai Time Out*

There are also countless jobs in rural Japan such as working on Japanese plum farms making *umeboshi* (sour pickles), making *himono* (dried fish) or picking fruit; all of which generally provide accommodation and meals in addition to a meagre wage. In a job like this you can count on attracting some attention to yourself.

Why work in these kinds of 'odd' jobs? For some, it's a chance to escape the English teaching scene; for others it offers the flexibility to work short-term contracts in different parts of Japan (a real 'working holiday'). It's almost impossible to generalise about these kinds of jobs: some are short-term, others long term; some require you to have a work visa, others may not; there are office jobs, outdoor jobs, jobs in the entertainment industry, others in building or labouring.

It's probably safe to say, however, that most of these jobs require at least some ability in Japanese, which might mean that you hold off looking until after you've been in Japan for some time and picked up som of the language and customs. Then again, your boss could be a *gaijin* too: after the 1995 Kobe earthquake, there was so much building work that *gaijin* builders, carpenters and other trades people moved to Kobe from all over Japan (some even flew to Japan especially for the well-paid work) and employed other *gaijin* to help them put the city back together.

How to find 'odd' jobs

- Use every available resource you can: ask other *gaijin* you know, check the classifieds in the newspapers and foreigners' magazines, and use the JAWHM notice board and website at www.mmjp.or.jp/jawhm/contents.htm since working holiday makers are often targetted for short-term jobs.

- *Kansai Time Out* and *Tokyo Time Out* tend to have the most ads offering more unusual, one-off jobs.

Taking it to the streets

For the ultimate in flexible work environments, busking and selling jewellery, paintings and crafts on the streets can be lucrative work in major cities where there's a big enough population to ensure a steady flow of customers, particularly at peak hours. You can be your own boss and work whatever hours you like. Just keep in mind that it may not be a year-round job unless you can brave the chill (even snow) of winter (January and February are the coldest months).

In some cities it's illegal to be a street vendor but if the police hassle you, the usual procedure is to apologise and move on, before discreetly setting up somewhere else. A more real and threatening presence is the *yakuza* (Japanese mafia). Since they tend to control most busy entertainment districts, they like to take a cut of anything happening on 'their turf'. You just have to get a feel for the place and get to know a few people in the area where you want to set up.

Every city has an entertainment district and you soon learn which are the busiest corners and arcades. Every city also has different restrictions on street performers. Your best bet is to go ahead and play and if someone stops you, plead ignorance. Playing your own songs, however, no matter how inspired they are, won't win you many fans in Japan. Trite as it may seem, playing crowd pleasers like the Beatles, Eric Clapton, the Eagles, Rolling Stones and—let's go way back there—John Denver, will please the crowds and earn you not only applause but a few thousand yen for a couple of hours playing. You might even get an offer to play in a club somewhere.

Some areas in each city give you more hassle than others. At first, just set up your battery-powered amps and go ahead and play. Probably because you're foreign there'll be someone who wants you to play at a bar close by. That's how it all starts. But don't expect to just come over here and make it straight away. Even if your band's played everywhere, it's hard. You've got to set up a regular job, or one of you [in the band] gets a regular job to support the rest. You can do it on your working holiday visa. Travel around and play, make lots of friends, they'll all put you up. It's quite possible. Vince Panero, an American musician who used to live in Fukuoka.

Sushi and sake

It's probably safe to say that your first Japanese experiences will have to do with food, and the world of Japanese food knows no limits. It might be dominated by fresh fish, other seafood and seasonal vegetables, but the range of dishes is almost infinite. If you're thinking expensive, forget it. If you're thinking raw fish and rice every day, forget that too.

Gaijin food

It takes time to adjust to eating Japanese food for every meal every day, so give yourself time to ease into it. Western foods like bread, steak, coffee, even French pastries, are readily available in all but the smallest villages. If you go into a Western-style restaurant you'll usually have to read *katakana* to decipher the menu and even then it can be a challenge. However, at fast food places like KFC, Pizza Hut, Mister Donut and Dunkin Donuts as well as Japan's own Lotteria and Mos Burger (which has the best made-to-order hamburgers that taste like real burgers) you can usually just point to the pictures on the menu.

There are also family restaurants such as Royal Host, Royal Butler, Ninjin Boy, Baal and Gusto which, in the tradition of Sizzlers, offer huge servings of such familiar things as bacon and eggs for breakfast and thick steaks for dinner, plus refillable cups of coffee as in American restaurants. Sometimes you'll see restaurants, usually those in big hotels, advertising 'Viking' or 'Biking' meals; this means smorgasbord (from the Scandinavian Vikings, is my guess).

European-style coffee shops (*kissaten*) are usually trendy, and because of this not usually cheap. A cup of coffee at such a place can set you back ¥500 and is usually served black with a small disposable container of milk. Fancy coffees like lattés and cappuccinos can generally only be found in coffee shops in major cities. Tea is also served black unless specified as lemon tea (with a slice of lemon in it), milk tea or iced tea. Most coffee shops close around 8 pm or 9 pm. Some offer cheap breakfasts. If you ask for the morning service (*moningu-sabisu*) between 7 am and 10 am you can get toast, salad, an egg, maybe a slice of processed meat and coffee or tea for around the price of a cup of coffee at other times of the day. You pay for the atmosphere at places like this but they do provide a private place for friends to meet, or for the occasional English lesson, and you can usually stay as long as you like on one cup of coffee or tea. A cheaper alternative is to buy your coffee for ¥120 from a vending machine; it comes in a can, cold in summer and hot in winter, with brands like Georgia Blend, UCC, Boss or Jive.

Restaurants specialising in foreign foods, such as Indian, Thai, Mexican, French or Italian, tend to be less common and more expensive than back home. The exception is Chinese—every town and suburb seems to have a cheap Chinese restaurant.

Visiting someone's home for dinner

Think of the last special dinner you had back home, in a restaurant or someone's home: the atmosphere, the lighting, there was probably music, perhaps a view, flowers or candles on the table, and most definitely a few drinks to stimulate the flow of conversation. In Japan, by contrast, the food takes centre stage, often to the exclusion of everything else, particularly in private homes (as opposed to restaurants).

The first time I really understood this was when I was invited by a Japanese friend to have dinner at the home of one of his well-to-do clients in the mountains of southern Kyushu. To this day it remains one of the most traditional (and unusual) dining experiences I've ever had. When we arrived the woman of the house greeted us at the door by getting down on her hands and knees and bowing her head to the floor (the deepest, most respectful bow imaginable) and throughout the meal she proceeded to shuffle between kitchen and dining room bringing out various exquisitely prepared (and delicious) dishes, but never actually partaking of any herself. The food was her gift to us, her contribution to the evening.

The room where we ate was completely bare, except for an ornate shrine in an alcove at one end, and it was cold. Four of us knelt in our socks and heavy jumpers at a low table, our hands almost too frozen to hold the chopsticks. There was no music. A single fluorescent tube hummed above our heads. No-one spoke except to offer more food or beer. And although it all felt strange to me, my Japanese friends seemed completely content to just eat, focussing on the food in front of them with no distractions.

Eating etiquette

Take a gift if eating at someone's home. It doesn't have to be anything expensive. It's quite acceptable to take flowers, fruit, some beer, or something from your home country.

Being complimented on your ability to eat with chopsticks (*o-hashi*) is par for the course. Although you may think being able to use chopsticks is nothing special, a lot of Japanese are still blown away by it and they're likely to comment on how well you do it. They'll usually say something like '*Jozu desu ne*!' or '*Umai desu ne*'. They're not taking the mickey out of you, they are genuinely impressed, or at the very least trying to put you at ease and make you feel welcome. As with any compliments in Japan, the best response is to smile graciously, shake your head and say '*Mada mada.*' ('I'm nowhere near expert yet.')

Chopstick etiquette is very important. In all but the most high class restaurants you'll be given a pair of disposable wooden chopsticks (*waribashi*). If you start thinking about the vast quantities of wood (often from Indonesian rainforests) used to make all the single-use chopsticks in Japan, you might like to BYO chopsticks and carry them around in a hygienic case. Be prepared for some flak if you do this (particularly stares), since this will be regarded as fairly radical behaviour. Don't stick your chopsticks upright in your rice: this signifies death because that's how rice is offered to the spirits of the dead. Don't pass food from your chopsticks to someone else's since this too is associated with death (in Buddhist rituals, this is how the dead person's bones are passed around the family). If you want to pass food to someone else, use the blunt end of your chopsticks, i.e. the end you don't eat from.

Giving compliments. If you want to say how much you're enjoying the food, simply say '*Oishii*!' ('Delicious!').

Food is generally served all at once, or at least in the order in which it was ordered. There's no entree, main and dessert courses. Different foods are normally served in different bowls so you can savour the individual flavour and texture of each. There are no hard and fast rules about what to eat first but rice is usually eaten alternately with other dishes or last. Green tea signifies the end of the meal.

Rice is sacred. The purity of it is very important. That's why it's usually served in a separate bowl. It's also why most Japanese won't add anything to their bowl of rice; it verges on sacrilegious to pour any kind of sauce over it. The uniqueness of Japanese rice has been argued for centuries, and many Japanese still won't touch foreign rice even though their own can be twice the price. It seems many would rather not eat rice at all than eat something they regard to be inferior. Japanese rice tends to be quite sticky, making it easy to eat with chopsticks.

How to eat difficult dishes. You can pick up bowls or dishes and push food into your mouth with your chopsticks. When eating noodles it's quite the done thing to slurp, in fact it's said to enhance the flavour by increasing the air flow as you take the noodles into your mouth, not to mention cooling them down. Soup is usually sipped from the bowl, using your chopsticks to pick up the seaweed, tofu and other bits at the bottom. There are certain sauces for certain foods: if in doubt about what goes with what, ask one of your dining companions or spy on another table to see what they're doing.

Before the meal people usually say '*Ita daki masu*' ('I gratefully accept this meal') and after the meal, '*Go chi so sama deshita*' ('Thank you for the lovely meal').

Beware! Certain Japanese foods can tickle the palate of even the most hardy *gaijin* and not always in a pleasant way. A few of the 'challenging' foods to watch out for are: *anko*, a sweet red bean paste that's put in everything from donuts to bread rolls; *wasabi*, a green horseradish condiment usually eaten with sushi (a little goes a long way); and *natto,* an infamous sticky soy bean paste which Japanese friends are bound to ask you to try.

Paying for the meal. If someone invites you to eat or drink, it usually means they're paying. It's unusual to divide up bills according to who ate and drank what. If they divide the bill up at all (usually when you're eating out with other young people and good friends) it'll be into equal portions with everyone paying the same amount. If you are being shouted to a meal, it's polite to at least make a gesture of trying to contribute to the bill.

Japanese fast food

A good place to start your culinary adventure is with takeaway food. It's quick, tasty and nutritious and there's no need to bother with etiquette. It can be cheaper than cooking at home, not to mention easier (at least until you work out how to use those ingredients you bought from your local Japanese supermarket). In fact if you live in a large city, chances are you'll be eating out for most, if not all, your main meals. A large part of your diet could consist of small meals eaten on the run. So here's the low-down of what you can expect to be eating if you want a snack or are in a hurry.

Onigiri is the Japanese equivalent of a sandwich and consists of a ball of rice with something tasty in the centre. They're made by pressing hot boiled rice between your hands, poking a filling into the centre (a plum, tuna, prawns, etc) and often wrapping it all in seaweed. They're eaten cold or hot, sold just about everywhere and cost about ¥120 for one the size of a flattened tennis ball.

O-bento or ***bento*** literally means 'lunch box' although they are often bought for dinner. *Bento* consists of rice and something else (chicken, beef, vegetables; or a noodle-based dish) in a box, traditionally wooden or lacquered, now more commonly plastic or polystyrene. Bento shops are usually hole-in-the-wall establishments with the boxes displayed under glass in the front counter. *Eki-ben* is *bento* sold at train stations. There are specialist chain *bento* stores like WE'SN and Hokka Hokka Tei, which you'll soon learn to spot by their colourful signs and flashing lights. They're often open late (11 pm), and some are open 24 hours. The cost of a *bento* dinner ranges from ¥350 for the most basic to ¥700 for the top of the line.

Noodles is such a fast food you often eat it standing up! The usual procedure at most noodle shops is to buy a coupon at a machine, and hand it to the waitress who then brings your bowl of noodles to you. The cheapest is about ¥400 – 500 a bowl. There are also vending machines selling 'cup *ramen*' noodles in a polystyrene cup for about ¥150.

Takoyaki literally means 'octopus dumplings' which are more appetising than their name suggests. The dumplings are made of flour, onion, ginger and chopped calimari. These are then fried and skewered on a bamboo stick and sold at family-owned shops and stalls at major tourist attractions. There's also a chain of *takoyaki* stores recognisable by the giant octopus sitting astride the roof (reminiscent for many Aussies of the Big Banana, the Big Prawn, the Big Merino etc). A box of four sticks costs about ¥400.

Okinomiyaki also goes by the name 'Osaka pancake' or 'Osaka pizza' because you can choose your own toppings and it's a specialty of the Kansai region. Most Osaka locals know how to make it, as it's so quick and easy. Start with a flour batter to which you add whatever you like (often leftovers if you're making it at home), e.g. diced seafood, vegetables, meat, tuna, egg, corn, cheese or bacon. Then fry it on both sides like a pancake on a hot plate. Sprinkle with *aonori* (green seaweed powder), *katsuo* (dried bonito fish shavings) and special *okinomiyaki* sauce. One very filling pancake costs about ¥650.

Oden is fish cake stew, and again is more appetising than it sounds. It's made by simmering assorted pieces of fish, dumplings, eggs, vegetables and fried *tofu* in a stock for a few hours. In winter, stalls selling *oden* line the main roads of entertainment districts and the streets near railway stations. The drill is to sit at the narrow counter and choose what you want from the pot.

Yatai are the pushcarts that ply the entertainment districts. They sometimes have a roof and stools so you can sit at the counter while you eat. They serve a range of dishes including most of the above, as well as the ubiquitous beers.

Home-delivered fast food. Some restaurants (mostly *sushi*, *soba* and Chinese food places) deliver meals to homes and offices in their local area. You can tell if a place delivers because it'll have its delivery bicycles or motorbikes with purpose-built carrier racks parked outside. They generally bring the food in their own enamel or ceramic plates and bowls. When you've finished eating, rinse the dishes, put them back on the tray they came with and leave them outside your door (or, if you live in an apartment block, in the foyer). To ask a restaurant if they deliver, say 'your area *made demae dekimasu ka.*'

Some common Japanese dishes

You've graduated to the next level of eating in Japan, traditional Japanese dishes. But before you go galloping off to the nearest *sushi* bar, it's worth familiarising yourself with the range of dishes available.

Sushi and ***sashimi***. To many outsiders, this is quintessential Japanese food. *Sushi* is usually raw seafood on a cushion of cold vinegared rice. It can also consist of rice and seafood wrapped in seaweed (*nori*), like a Swiss roll which is then cut into discs. *Sushi* actually refers to the use of flavoured rice, not the rawness of the fish. *Sashimi* is raw seafood served without the rice. It's made by slicing boneless, skinless fillets of certain fish (usually tuna, sea bream, cuttlefish, bonito, flathead and shellfish) into bite-sized pieces.

Packs of fresh *sushi* and *sashimi* can be bought at convenience stores and supermarkets as a cheap lunch, for about ¥300 – 400. There are also places called *kaiten zushi* where you sit at a counter and take pieces of *sushi* as they go past on a conveyor belt. *Sashimi* tends to be more expensive than *sushi*. One special type of *sashimi* is *fugu* or blowfish, which is poisonous unless it's prepared properly by a licensed chef. Even then its season is only between October and March. It's also very expensive and so for wealthy daredevils only.

At a *sushi* restaurant, you'll often sit at the counter and chat to the chef while he prepares your meal. It's considered part of his job and many a good *sushi* restaurant gains its reputation at least partly from the personality and charm of its chefs. Plus it's interesting to see the little tricks they use, like dipping their fingers in cold vinegar while working, to keep the fish fresh and hygienic, and working quickly so the fish doesn't heat up in their hands. *Sushi* restaurants, perhaps more than any other Japanese restaurants, are for eating and it's considered impolite to stay long after you've finished eating. If you do stay it will be assumed that you want to order more dishes.

When eating *sushi* or *sashimi* add a little *wasabi* to your dish of soy sauce. The *wasabi* is thought to stimulate the taste buds and have a sterilising effect on the fish. When eating *sushi*, make sure you turn it upside down (with the rice on top) before dipping it in the sauce otherwise the rice will come unstuck and you'll end up with half your *sushi* in the soy sauce dish or in your lap (speaking from experience). To eat *sashimi*, simply pick up a piece of fish with your chopsticks and dip it in the dish of soy sauce.

Tempura refers to the deep frying of vegetables, seafood and meat. The batter is a simple flour, egg and water mix. There are many variations including *tendon* (*tempura* on a bed of rice) and *tempura-udon* (*tempura* on top of Japanese wheat noodles). This is a common dinner dish, best eaten when hot. The names of *tempura* restaurants usually begin with *ten-*.

Nabemono is the word for anything cooked in a pot at the table. *Sukiyaki* and *shabu-shabu* are the two best known cook-in-the-pot dishes. Perfect for dinner on cold winter nights with friends, *nabemono* warms you up and provides a good atmosphere for family and friends to socialise, as everyone sits around and eats from the communal pot. At a restaurant, usually a platter of raw ingredients is brought to your table and everyone cooks their own favourite things in the pot. A gas burner is often set into the table top. *Sukiyaki* consists of thin slices of beef which simmer with vegetables (spring onions, *tofu*, *shiitake* mushrooms and cabbage) in a broth of soy sauce, *sake*, sugar and chrysanthemum leaves. *Shabu-shabu* has its name from the sound made when you swish the sliced beef around in the pot with your chopsticks. It's almost the same as *sukiyaki* except you cook *shabu-shabu* yourself in a doughnut-shaped pot and dip the cooked food in special sauces, one citrus flavoured, another thicker and sesame-based.

Yakimono means 'grilled things'. *Yakiniku* is grilled beef and consists of thinly sliced beef (or liver, tongue and kidneys if they take your fancy) which is grilled on a hot plate at your table. Usually four to six people sit at one table, with a chimney overhead to take away the smoke. *Yakitori* is chicken pieces grilled over hot charcoal, giving it a distinctive flavour. You can recognise a *yakitori-ya* ('grilled chicken shop') by the small red lanterns outside and the smoke billowing out of the kitchen vent (which often opens directly into the street in order to tempt passers-by with the aromas). These have a very casual atmosphere, since both *yakiniku* and *yakitori* are usually eaten with cold beer.

Teppanyaki literally means 'grilled steak' so *teppanyaki-ya* are the Japanese equivalent of steakhouses. Dining at one is usually as entertaining as it is nourishing, you've probably even been to one back home. The chef cooks at your table, or rather you dine at his hotplate. As he flings and chops and turns over the meat and other assorted ingredients with a flash of razor sharp knives and spatulas, the diners 'ooh' and 'aah' at his expertise (that and the fact that he still manages to have all his fingers). Not surprisingly, all this entertainment doesn't come cheap—partly because beef is still something of a luxury in Japan—so *teppanyaki-ya* tend to be frequented by businessmen entertaining their clients.

Miso-shiru is *miso* soup traditionally drunk straight from a lacquered bowl (which usually comes to the table with a lid to keep it hot). The traditional Japanese breakfast consists of a bowl of rice, a few pickles and some *miso* soup. *Miso* is soybean paste (made from crushed soy beans with salt and a fungus that causes the paste to mature over the years) to which you add hot water and one or two ingredients like *tofu*, mushrooms and eggplant. You can make it yourself by buying the *miso* paste at the supermarket; there are also packets of instant *miso* which only require hot water.

Noodles are great and filling and there's a huge variety that are delicacies in their own right. *Ramen* (yellow egg noodles), originally from China, is the commonest and cheapest noodle. Often eaten on the run at noodle bars, *ramen* is a popular late night snack since most *ramen* places are open late and it's said that eating a bowl of *ramen* on your way home from a big night out will prevent a hangover the next morning. There are three main kinds of *ramen*, depending on the base used for the soup: *miso, shoyu* (soy sauce) or *shio* (salt). *Udon* (thick wheat noodles) are served hot and are a staple food of most Japanese. The dough (made from wheat flour with a little salt and water) is kneaded like bread dough and cut into long thin strips which are then cooked quickly in boiling water flavoured by various seasonal and regional vegetables. *Udon* is particularly filling and satisfying in winter. *Somen* (fine white noodles) is a traditional summer dish with the noodles served in a communal bowl with ice cubes. You use your chopsticks to remove them from the bowl and dip them in a cold sauce. *Soba* (buckwheat noodles) is served hot or cold and you dip the noodles in a thin sauce.

Tonkatsu is deep-fried pork in breadcrumbs. A cheap, filling, everyday meal, *tonkatsu* is usually eaten as part of a set meal (*teishoku*) with *miso* soup, rice, pickles and shredded raw cabbage.

Domburi is a bowl of rice with various cooked ingredients on top. There's chicken and egg (*oyakudon*) and beef (*nikudon* or *gyudon*) varieties.

Ocha is Japanese green tea but there are several types. The tea contains caffeine and was originally drunk by Zen Buddhist monks to help them stay awake whilst meditating. *Kocha* is ordinary (Western) tea, *mugicha* is barley tea and is drunk cold while *oolong cha* is a Chinese tea. An almost endless range of teas is available at vending machines.

Eating out

How to find a reasonably priced restaurant

- Prices of food depend to a large extend on the location of the restaurant. Japan is said to have some of the most expensive real estate in the world so if you're on a budget, go for the places in the back streets. The food will be as good as on the main drag, but you won't be paying through the nose to subsidise the rent. Also, since Japan is such a safe, clean country, the back streets are still safe, the patrons honest and the food hygienically prepared. In fact, in Japan even the street stalls are clean. Cheap areas to eat out in Tokyo include Sukiyabashi (near the Ginza), Yutenji and Yuracho (on the Hibiya subway line), and Shibuya and Harajuku on the JR Yamanote line.

- Beware of restaurants that look very traditional, particularly those with stone lanterns out the front, Japanese gardens amidst groves of bamboo and maybe a trickling waterfall, as they tend to be pricey. In fact the waitstaff might even turn you away, anticipating that you won't be able to pay. Don't be offended: do yourself a favour and take their advice. An exception to this rule are those places with a red lantern outside. These are usually *izakayas*, *yakiniku* or *rabatayaki*. Also, if a restaurant has separate *tatami* rooms for private groups of diners, it's probably going to be more expensive. Look for those places with menu prices displayed outside and plastic food models in the window.

- Most department stores have a restaurant or two on their top floor. The tops of office blocks in large cities can also have restaurants with great views. In any town, the areas around (and under) train stations and in shopping arcades are generally the best places to find affordable restaurants.

- It's cheaper to eat your main meal for lunch than for dinner, but try to avoid the lunch rush (usually between noon and 1 pm) when most office workers have their lunch break.

At the restaurant. You can tell if a restaurant is open by the split cloth curtain (*noren*) hung over the front door: if the cloth is hanging freely the restaurant is open and if it's tucked into the door, it's closed. It's quite common for restaurants in Japan to specialise in a particular dish. Although each place may serve other types of food, you'll get the best *tempura* at a *tempura* place and the best *sashimi* at a *sashimi* place. You can usually tell what kind of food they serve by the plastic replicas of dishes displayed in their front window.

Once in, you will be greeted with '*Irasshaimase!*' ('Welcome!') to which you just say '*Konnichiwa*' or '*Konbanwa*' (depending on the time of day). You sit down either on a *tatami* mat or chairs and will be given a hot or cold damp towel (*oshibori*) to wipe your hands. The waiter might take it away or leave it for you to wipe your fingers on during the meal (a necessity especially when eating *sushi*, as there's usually no serviettes). On the table, you'll usually find a bottle or dish of soy sauce (*shoyu*) and containers of disposable chopsticks and toothpicks.

Many restaurants have a glass display cabinet out the front containing plastic replicas of all the dishes they serve. These replicas look so real—professional chefs are consulted in their design—they have become collectors' items. You can even buy a model of your favourite dish from restaurant suppliers. If you can't read the menu simply take the waiter outside, point to the model of what you want and say '*kore o hitotsu kudasai*'('one of these please').

The next simplest way to order is to ask for the set meal of the day (*teishoku*) which is generally reasonably priced and consists of a main dish, rice, *miso* soup, pickles and some raw cabbage. To ask the waiter what they recommend (handy when you can't read the menu and there are no plastic models!) say, '*O-susume wa nan desu ka.*' To expand your repertoire of dishes, it's a good idea to learn *katakana*, the national restaurant language (at least it seems that way). At the other end of the spectrum, some places have no menu, just the names of their dishes written in *gaijin*-proof *kanji* on vertical strips of paper or cloth tacked to the walls. To go to those places you'll need to bring a Japanese friend or *kanji*-proficient *gaijin*.

Most restaurants have a fairly high turnover of customers, to keep their prices down, so it's best not to linger over your meal. You sit down, you order and the food comes without too much delay; then you eat, pay and leave. The Japanese tend not to have coffee or dessert, instead they drink green tea to signify the end of the meal. The bill (*o-kanjo*) is usually brought to your table with the last dish you ordered. When you're ready to go, take the bill to the front desk and pay. If you're in a group the waiter might ask if you'll be paying together (*issho*) or separately (*betsu betsu*). Don't leave a tip: it's not the done thing and the response will usually be one of either embarrassment or confusion (or both!).

Drinking

Drinking is an important part of Japanese (not to mention *gaijin*) culture. As in any country, it reinforces social bonds, particular those between work colleagues. It's not uncommon to see groups of businessmen enter a bar perfectly sober and even looking somewhat bored, only to emerge a few hours later completely transformed, talking loudly and jovially to each other, perhaps still singing the songs they sang in *karaoke*.

Traditionally drinking time used to be separate from eating time (drink first, eat later) but this isn't such a common approach these days, particularly since eating is often used as an excuse to drink! The official drinking age in Japan is 20, although it doesn't seem to be enforced: beer and spirits are widely available from vending machines and supermarkets. Public drunkenness is tolerated except when it comes to driving. Drink driving is a serious offence in Japan and the acceptable blood alcohol limit is *zero*.

A few drinking rules:

- Never pour your own drink and remember to always top up your drinking companions' glasses. When someone else is filling your glass it's polite to hold your glass up off the table. If someone offers you a drink from their *sake* decanter, drain your cup first before holding it out.

- If you want to stop drinking, you'll generally have to do it with a full glass in front of you. The moment you take a sip it's a sign that you're still in the game and your fellow drinkers will keep refilling your glass (which makes it very easy to lose track of how many drinks you've had). So if you leave your glass full they can't keep topping it up. You can try putting your hand over the glass when someone tries to refill it but this is often met with loud protests, until you remove your hand, such is the lure of a partially empty glass.

- The Japanese usually eat when they drink, so Japanese bars will often expect you to order at least some *otsumami* or *otoshi* (snacks) while you drink. Often they'll bring some over whether you've ordered them or not and add it to your bill (only about ¥100 – 200 per person).

- BYO seems to be an alien concept in Japan.
- *Kampai*! means Cheers!

What to drink

Beer (*biru*) is now the most popular drink in Japan. You can buy beer anywhere: every restaurant, supermarket and convenience store; even vending machines, which close around 11 pm (although it's often easy to find one they've forgotten to switch off!). There are huge 2 L cans and tiny 100 ml cans but the standard size costs about ¥220. Draft beer is called *nama biru*. Beer is usually served in large mugs or smaller glasses. As with food, the price of a beer depends on the venue and can be anywhere between ¥400 for a small glass and ¥1200 for a litre in a beer garden (the average price for a mug of beer is ¥600). Local brands include Kirin, Asahi, Suntory and Sapporo.

Sake (pronounced 'sa-kay') is the national drink. This fermented rice wine can be drunk hot or cold and is around 17% alcohol, but is more potent when hot. *Sake* is sold in large bottles at liquor shops, or in smaller glass containers from vending machines. At restaurants it's served in small ceramic cups which cost around ¥250.

Shocchu is a vodka-like spirit made from sweet potatoes or wheat, containing around 30% alcohol and once used as a cleaning agent in the Edo Period! It's said to produce the worst hangovers. You can drink it as *oyuwari* (diluted with hot water) or *chuhai* (mixed with lemon squash or other soft drink).

Spirits include whisky (*uisuki*), which is by far the most popular spirit among the Japanese and is usually served as *mizuwari* (with water and ice). Suntory is the most popular brand and costs about ¥500 – 700 for a shot (imported brands are more expensive). Other mixed drinks, such as rum and Coke, are only available at nightclubs and large bars, for about ¥500 – 800.

Wine is mostly imported and served in wine bars, *teppanyaki* restaurants and Western restaurants. It's not as popular as back home.

Non-alcoholic drinks include most of those we know and love (Coke, Pepsi, Fanta, Mountain Dew, 7 Up) as well as bottled water, fruit juices and a few you won't have heard of. These include isotonic 'sports' drinks such as Pocari Sweat, Calpis Water and Aquarius, and *genki* drinks (containing various quantities of vitamins, caffeine and sugar) to give you a hit when you're tired. A standard can costs ¥120 from vending machines. Soft drinks (and sometimes cocktails and spirits) are often free at nightclubs and bars once you pay the cover charge.

Where to drink

Beer gardens are generally open-air and used in summer only. They're usually located on the rooftops of high buildings such as office blocks, high rise hotels and department stores. In winter the beer garden crowd migrates to *izakaya* (see below).

Bars include several types of establishments. The most typical are the very small bars, often the size of an average Western living room, with space for maybe 10 to 20 people. They're so intimate you can feel like you're intruding if you walk in off the street without knowing any of the regular customers or the barman. The entertainment districts are full of such bars often stacked on top of each other in four or five storey buildings. Competition for regular patrons is so strong that bar owners have invented the 'keep bottle' system to lure customers back night after night: you buy a bottle of your favourite liquor from the bar, they write your name on it and keep it behind the bar for you so that every time you go back to that bar you can have your drinks poured from your own bottle and only pay an 'ice charge'.

It's easier to be a stranger in larger places and most foreigners' bars fall into this category. The major cities have numerous foreigners' bars and nightclubs. You usually pay a cover charge (around ¥3000 – 4000) which includes at least one 'complimentary' drink of spirits and one or two beers. In Osaka there's Murphy's Irish Pub, the Pig and Whistle, and Bar Isn't It; in Tokyo there's a Hard Rock Cafe in Roppongi and countless other pubs. Check the foreigners' press for details, locations, gigs, special events and parties. A new Hard Rock Cafe opened in Fukuoka early in 2000 with lots of foreign waitstaff and fancy albeit pricey cocktails.

Snack (pronounced 'su-na-kku') are Japanese-style bars. They tend to be more expensive than those mentioned above because of their extra offerings: hostesses, *karaoke* and a 'keep bottle' system.

Izakaya and *Nomiya* both mean 'drinking-shop' and are casual places offering cheap drinks and a wide range of snacks. They range from cosy, traditional, family-owned bars frequented by regulars, to larger beer halls frequented by young people (especially university students). They tend to be very noisy and only serve beer, *shocchu* and whisky.

Robatayaki-ya are like *izakaya* but specialise in charcoal-grilled foods which are usually cooked in front of you. They usually have traditional farmhouse-style decor.

Aka chochin means 'red lantern' and these are small neighbourhood pubs recognisable by the red paper lantern hanging out the front. They usually serve noodles and beer, and are often located in the back streets near suburban train stations.

Nightclubs are plentiful and mainly for dancing as well as drinking. You usually have to pay a cover charge of around ¥3000. Most cities have a live music scene with a wide range of music styles. Check the foreigners' press for details of these and any touring bands—most international acts put Japan on their tour schedule (at least Tokyo, Osaka and Fukuoka). There's also an array of hostess bars, cocktail bars, hotel lounges, cabarets and clubs with performers. Plenty to choose from.

In search of the 'real' Japan

Much of travelling in any country is a search for the essence of that country. So what is the 'real' Japan and where do you find it? To me it's Japan undiluted by Western influences—like a village with no signs in English—but the 'real' Japan can be so many other things. It can be something you see, somewhere you go, an experience, an image, a feeling. It can be a girl wearing a *kimono* clip-clopping along a busy street in Osaka in her *geta* (traditional wooden sandals). Or a sound, like the distinctive ding-ding-ding signal at my local rail crossing, or the tinkle of the little wind chime a friend bought for me in Kyoto. It can be as simple as sleeping on a *futon* every night and eating white rice with every meal. It can even be doing things you couldn't do back home, or anywhere else in the world, like spending a night in a love hotel.

The 'real' Japan can also be something more familiar like riding the 'bullet train,' climbing Mt Fuji, singing *karaoke*, watching a *sumo* match or visiting a thousand-year-old shrine. It can be a rare event that you've had the opportunity to witness: like the time I was invited to watch a traditional all-night dance, the *kagura*, in an old farmhouse in Kyushu in the middle of winter; the whole town gathered in someone's house and we all shared blankets and bottles of *sake* to ward off the cold.

Top 12 'real' Japan experiences

Love in a capsule

Two of the most original accommodation options in the world, love hotels and capsule hotels, offer more than just accommodation.

Love hotels are fantastic, crazy places where couples can escape behind closed doors for a few hours of intimacy (not necessarily sex, though there are ample accessories provided including videos, vibrating beds, water beds and vending machines selling sex aids). They definitely have a niche in the market and are often frequented by married couples just wanting some space. Remember most people in Japan's major cities don't have a car at their disposal and 'home' is either too far away or filled to the brim with kids and aunties.

You can always tell the love hotels from any other kind of hotel: they're the ones with the medieval castle turrets, Rapunzelesque towers and space-age rockets, or they might have UFO decor or look like a Mediterranean villa. The crazier and more fun they look, the better.

Love hotels may not be sleazy but they are nevertheless discreet. The entrance and exit are usually separate, and when you walk into the lobby you're met by a lighted board, much like a vending machine showing pictures of all the rooms available and their prices, so you don't have to see another human being on your way to your room. Most love hotels have various 'theme' rooms, for example, a jungle room or a Roman room, and there's always one with wall-to-wall and ceiling mirrors. You press the button corresponding to the room you want, go over to the reception desk (which will often be nothing more than a slot in the wall) where you anonymously pay and receive the room key. Sometimes you don't pay until after your stay; instead you take a key from the lighted panel of your choice in the foyer and a series of flashing lights set into the floor will lead you down the hall to your room where there might be a timer counting down the amount of time you have left before someone comes knocking on the door demanding 'check out-o'.

There are two room rates. 'Rest' rates allow you to take a room on an hourly basis. Peak times are during the day and early evening. Most couples go for two hours, which costs about ¥3000. 'Stay' rates are for overnight and if you wait until 9 pm or 10 pm, you can stay the night for as little as ¥5000 per room (up to ¥9000 per room in major cities) which makes love hotels some of the cheapest overnight accommodation in Japan.

At the opposite end of the romantic spectrum you'll find **capsule hotels**. The first capsule hotel was a series of modified shipping containers fitted with a bed, bath and all 'mod cons'. A place for weary business travellers (and those who missed the last train home) but much cheaper than other available accommodation.

Today's capsules measure 2 m x 1 m x 1 m, making them more like a berth on a ship than a spacious shipping container (not recommended if you have any tendencies to claustrophobia). In that space you have a single bed, TV, reading light, radio, alarm clock and air conditioning. There are no windows, most capsules being stacked two or three high and side-by-side taking up a whole wall. Pyjamas and slippers are provided and you store your clothes, bags and briefcases in a locker down the hall. There's usually a communal bath, and often a sauna, coffee shop, TV lounge and restaurant, even a laundry.

The only catch is that most capsule hotels are for men only. There are a few for women only and some that have private rooms for two or four people, but there are no mixed capsule hotels. The capsules can't be locked, even from the inside (for safety reasons). The average price of a capsule is ¥4000 per night or you can have a nap for around ¥1500 for three hours (not common).

Riding the 'bullet'

Only foreigners call the *shinkansen* the 'bullet train'. Reaching speeds of up to 270 km/h, the *shinkansen* was the world's first high speed train when it began operation in 1964 (the TGV in France opened in 1981 and the German ICE only started up in 1991) but it's no longer the world's fastest—that honour goes to the French TGV, though the new German ICE 3 looks set to overtake even that with speeds clocked around 305 km/h.

The *shinkansen* looks like a flightless aircraft, and inside it even feels like one as it glides noiselessly over seamless tracks laid from one end of Japan to the other. It has a safety record to rival that of Qantas and there are hostesses (we can't call them flight attendants) serving a variety of food and drinks, though unfortunately these aren't complimentary. There are announcements in English and Japanese and you can get English timetables and route maps at most major stations and any Tourist Information Centre. You can buy *shinkansen* tickets at any travel agent or JR ticket office.

There are four main *shinkansen* routes:

- The Tokkaido Route: Tokyo-Nagoya-(past Mt Fuji)-Kyoto-Osaka-Hiroshima-Shimonoseki. This route is by far the most scenic

- The Tohoku Route: Tokyo-Sendai-Morioka (in north-eastern Honshu). You can branch off at Morioka for Akita. From Fukushima (near Sendai) you can also branch off to Yamagata and Shinjo

- The Nagano Shinkansen: Tokyo-Nagano (ski fields)

- The Joetsu Route: Tokyo-Niigata (north of Tokyo)

Climbing Mt Fuji

On your way past Mt Fuji on the *shinkansen*, you might spare a thought for the hordes of climbers who trek up to its 3776 m summit every summer. Mt Fuji, Fuji-yama or Fuji-san is more than Japan's highest mountain. It's been a cultural icon for centuries, a symbol of the 'real' Japan to outsiders and locals alike. Who hasn't seen the postcards and guidebook covers depicting the *shinkansen* speeding past a snow-capped Mt Fuji?

During the warmer months when its volcanic slopes are free of snow, Mt Fuji lures up to 180,000 people per year. The official climbing season is July and August but you can climb Fuji any time except mid-winter, when the four to five hour hike becomes a serious mountaineering expedition. There are 10 stations between the base and summit, but you can drive or take a bus to the fifth (there are actually several fifth stations on various sides of the mountain), so most climbers start from there.

Climbing Fuji is literally a once-in-a-lifetime experience. As the saying goes, 'You're a fool if you never climb Mt Fuji, but you're an even bigger fool if you climb it twice!' To understand this, you only have to talk to someone who's done it (whilst making sure they don't put you off attempting it once). It's dusty and slippery, the volcanic gravel making you do the old one-step-forward-two-steps-back shuffle, particularly if you've hiked up in the dark to get there by dawn. If you're looking to get back to nature, this is not the climb for you. In summer it's crowded with everyone from school groups to elderly grandparents, the paths are lined with drink vending machines and there's even a souvenir shop balanced precariously on the crater rim. One volcanic shudder and down it would go, Fuji film and all, into the crater itself (not such a far out idea since Fuji is still classified as an active volcano). But, if nothing else, climbing Fuji is a great people-watching exercise, a glimpse at what the Japanese do in their free time.

Home sweet home

Where else can you find the real Japan if not in the homes of the locals? Not all homes are traditional, of course, but then that's 'real' too because Japan is, as you will have learned by now, a mix (even a clash) of old and new, tradition and modernity.

You will be asked into people's homes, no doubt about it. However, if you want to have some experience of Japanese homes in different parts of Japan, the Home Visit Scheme is a great way to go. This program allows you to visit a Japanese family for a few hours in the evening, usually after dinner. There are about 900 families who take in foreign guests free of charge, spread across 14 cities including Narita, Tokyo, Yokohama, Nagoya, Otsu, Kyoto, Osaka, Kobe, Kurashiki, Okayama, Hiroshima, Fukuoka, Kumamoto and Miyazaki. Most host families speak English; some speak French, German and other languages as well. To take part in the program you can only apply in Japan, in person, and you should apply at least one day in advance, at your nearest Tourist Information Centre or the tourist office in the area you would like to visit (ask the JNTO for a list of tourist offices before you leave home). You can only do one home visit during your stay in Japan.

Then there's homestays. Here you stay in a Japanese family's home and live with them as part of the family (which includes helping with chores). The stay can be from a few days to several months, the aim being a cultural experience for you and for them (they get to meet and live with a *gaijin*). The JAWHM can organise one for about ¥25 – 50,000 per month including three meals.

Natural Japan

The Japanese have a great love of nature, and you don't have to go far to find evidence of that. From the 'Flower of the Week' on the front page of one of the national newspapers, to the average person knowing the scientific names for more species of flora and fauna that you can poke a stick at, to their festivals celebrating phases of the moon or the blossoming of cherries.

Then there's their penchant for hiking. Japan being such a mountainous country, it's easy to say the Japanese have little choice but to love their mountains. But whatever the reason, they seem to get out there at every opportunity.

One autumn, at the top of a volcano in Kirishima National Park in Kyushu, some *gaijin* friends and I got talking to a man who looked like he'd just hiked out of a mountain sports catalogue, right down to his gaiters and cotton gloves. He'd been coming to the mountains every Monday (his day off) for the last 15 years, and offered to take us on one of his favourite tracks. Five hours later, with aching legs and shoes covered in mud, we all arrived back at the bottom of the mountain (the walk up had only taken an hour). But far from complaining, we were grateful. He'd devoted his whole day to showing us 'his' mountain, letting us ride on his coat-tails (so to speak) and seeing the national park through his eyes. He told us about a tree that was used for making candle wicks and another that was used for making pimple-removing cream (our guide was a beautician by trade), that this lake was in the 007 movie *Goldfinger,* and explained why the leaves weren't so colourful this autumn. But the main thing I learned that day was his simple love of nature.

If the concept of Japanese wilderness seems like an oxymoron, head to Hokkaido. Only 5% of Japan's population lives there, and it's regarded as the outdoor mecca of Japan—a place where you can hike, climb, cycle, ski, go whitewater rafting and soak in natural springs, or pursue quieter activities such as nature photography and bird-watching, all amidst striking mountain scenery. Hokkaido is joined to the northern tip of Honshu by the Saikan tunnel (at 54 km, it's the world's longest undersea tunnel). This is a train tunnel only, which explains why, when I drove up to the souvenir shop in the little town near the southern end asking for road directions to the tunnel entrance, I was virtually hurled out of the store by gales of laughter from both the staff and customers.

Tokyo, of course

You can't go to Japan and not go to Tokyo. The sheer size and energy of this city (more than 12 million people live in an area covering about 2000 km²) makes it an enticing destination and just being there is an experience, rather than simply a sightseeing mission.

Unlike Western cities which often have a city centre surrounded by suburban sprawl, Tokyo actually consists of several distinct areas, each of which could be called a city in its own right. There's Akihabara, the discount electronics centre; the Ginza, which is the main shopping and commercial area where you'll also find the Imperial Palace and the Tokyo Tourist Information Centre; and Ueno, one of the older 'downtown' centres. Shinjuku is so large it's divided into east and west: East Shinjuku is a vast shopping and entertainment district while West Shinjuku is where you'll find some of the world's tallest buildings, which are home to Japanese top bureaucrats and businessmen. There's even a Disneyland on Tokyo's outskirts.

Ye olde Japan

Ah, Japan, the land of contrasts. Just when you've gone as far into the futuristic, high tech world as you can, it's time to do a backflip and land with both feet firmly planted on the cobbled square of one of Japan's most ancient temples.

There are several places where you can explore 'the old Japan'. You could safely start with Nara, south of Kyoto, since it was the first capital of Japan and is small enough to walk around in a day. But it's hard to go past Kyoto, with its plethora of ancient temples, beautifully laid out palaces and classic raked pebble gardens.

Although Kyoto overflows with about 40 million tourists a year its attractions are numerous enough—more than 1600 Buddhist temples and 300 Shinto shrines, as well as palaces and gardens—to prevent them all converging on the same place at the same time. And even if you do find yourself confronted with a mass of humanity (which can be part of the experience) it's never hard to find an escape route nearby, off the itineraries of the main tour groups, such as a quiet garden or shrine all to yourself.

But you don't have to go to Kyoto, Nara or Nikko (near Tokyo) to experience Japan's historical and cultural side. At Kyoto-kan, a new exhibition and information centre in the heart of Tokyo, you can view all Japan's traditional attractions in a matter of hours, including Japanese tea ceremony and demonstrations of traditional arts and crafts. For details call (03) 3560 3336.

Then there are the lesser known traditional places sprinkled all over Japan. Since Japan was once a mass of districts, virtually every village has its own sacred place. Like Europe's churches and cathedrals, they can provide a welcome relief from the commotion of modern Japanese life.

One of my favourite places (always on the 'tour' whenever any of my Australian friends visited) was Udo Shrine, which is built into a natural cave on Kyushu's south-eastern coast. Natural stone steps lead you down to its entrance, and on a sunny day it's a photographer's dream come true: the red shrine contrasting with a summer-blue ocean. From inside the cave you can hear the swell pounding against the rock walls below. But best of all, it has its very own myth. According to legend, one of Japan's earliest gods married the Princess Dragon of the Sea and when she became pregnant, she needed a place on dry land to give birth. So she rode up into this cave on the back of a giant turtle (which explains the large turtle-shaped rock near the cave's entrance) and instructed her husband not to look at her while she gave birth. Of course, as any good story would have it, he did look and discovered she was more dragon than princess. She then fled back to the sea, leaving their newborn son (who would later father Japan's first emperor) and her own breasts (so he wouldn't starve) embedded in the back wall of the cave (the locals assure me you can still see them today).

Temple stays (*shukubo*) offer you the chance to live like a Zen Buddhist monk for a few days. Most Zen temples require you to speak some Japanese (the ones in Kyoto are most likely to speak English) and often there are rules like no smoking or drinking. Some also offer Zen meditation tuition. There are *shukubo* in Tokyo and Kyoto but one of Japan's most important religious sites (and one of the most popular places to experience temple life) is Koyasan temple complex at Mt Koya, just south of Osaka, with more than 60 historical temples offering accommodation. A stay in a temple usually costs about ¥5000 per person per night (¥9000 – 15,000 at Koyasan) including two meals. For details contact Koyasan Tourist Association on (0736) 56 2616 or a travel agent.

Simply *sumo*

To say that *sumo* is Japan's national sport doesn't really convey the ... er ... weight of *sumo* in contemporary Japanese culture. *Sumo* champions are nothing short of national heroes, with the top-ranked wrestler being awarded the title of *Yokozuna* or grand champion.

Despite first impressions, *sumo* is a sport of great skill and technique, much of it lying in the psyching-out technique at the beginning of each bout and the anticipation of the opponent's moves. There are more than 70 official holds and manoeuvres but you soon learn to recognise different wrestlers' styles and abilities. The wrestlers do battle on a raised platform made of mud and sand, inside a rope circle. The aim of each wrestler is to unbalance his opponent so that he either steps out of the ring or touches the ground with part of his body other than the soles of his feet. Each bout lasts no more than 10 seconds. An excellent and very funny introduction to *sumo* is the 1994 movie *Sumo Do, Sumo Don't* (in Japanese, with English subtitles).

Sumo apparently began as a form of gladiatorial entertainment for the imperial court. Nowadays, watching a *sumo* match is part of almost everyone's daily life. In fact it's hard to escape the media coverage when a tournament is on. NHK, the national TV station, televises the bouts from 4 pm to 6 pm every day and the commercial stations show the highlights every night.

To see a *sumo* match in the flesh you can go to a tournament match or a practice session. There are six tournaments (*basho*) each year, each one lasting 15 days. Three are held in January, May and September at Tokyo's Shinkokugikan Stadium at Ryogoku. The other three are held in March (in Osaka), July (Nagoya) and November (Fukuoka). Tournaments usually start around 10 am, with the junior wrestlers (wearing plain brown cotton *mawashi*) going through their bouts. The higher level bouts (where the wrestlers wear brightly coloured *mawashi*) start around 3 pm and go until around 6 pm. A good way to see the wrestlers up close is to wait outside their dressing rooms for them to come out.

To buy tickets, queue up at the box office at the *sumo* stadium (ask at the TIC for locations) before 9 am on the day you want to go. You can also buy tickets from Lawson convenience stores and some travel agents such as JTB. Prices start at ¥2100 for an unreserved bench seat and go up to ¥11,300 for a piece of *tatami* mat in a prestige box. Ringside seats are virtually impossible to get since they're permanently booked by major corporations.

You can also watch the wrestlers training at their 'stables'. Most of the 60-odd stables are in the Ryogoku district in Tokyo. This is a chance to see the wrestlers close-up and actually be a guest in their 1500-year-old household. Best of all, it's free. Training usually takes place in the mornings from 5 am or 7 am until 10.30 am and no more than five visitors are allowed to watch at any one time. There's no training on the day before a tournament; and wrestlers take a weeks holiday after every tournament. Two Tokyo stables that have practice sessions open to the public are: Azumazeki-beya (Tel. [03] 3625 0033); and Takesago-beya (Tel. [03] 3876 8806) where Konishiki, the famous Hawaiian wrestler used to train. Phone first to book your visit.

Japan's island life

One part of Japan that often escapes mention when one thinks of the typical Japan is its island culture. There are more than 3000 islands in the Japanese archipelago, many of them too small to even be dots on the map.

The south-west islands in particular, which extend like stepping stones over an area stretching more than 1000 km from Kyushu to just off the coast of Taiwan, provide a glimpse of Japan that you'd never see on the 'mainland'. For hundreds of years the people of Okinawa, the best known of these islands, have considered themselves culturally separate from the rest of Japan, and have felt resentment towards the central government for its treatment of the island during the Second World War and afterwards. Okinawa was occupied by US Forces until as late as 1972 and still has the largest US military base outside America.

Other well known islands in this group are Yakushima and Tanegashima, Miyako-jima and the Yaeyama islands. One Golden Week holiday an American friend and I went to Yakushima for a break from our English teaching routine. Despite our poor command of the language (which became even poorer in the face of *Yakushima-ben*, the local dialect) and the fact that we knew virtually nothing about the island, we found ourselves having a cultural experience much deeper than any we could have planned. Camping and hitchhiking around the island we met like-minded Japanese campers and those touring by bicycle or motorbike, themselves trying to escape city life for a few days. Other tourists would pick us up in their hire cars and we'd visit the local attractions together; at one waterfall we found ourselves taking snapshots with two young women on holiday as if we'd known each other for years. Then there were the locals, country people who would stop to chat or give us a few *mikan* (small mandarins) as we trudged through their town with packs on our backs.

Local festivals

Unlike their highly publicised and often flamboyant cousins (the national festivals), local festivals (*matsuri*) offer a great opportunity to actually become part of Japan's culture for a few hours. Instead of feeling like you're watching a stream of mannequins parading past you in perfect time, the line between participants and spectators blurs. Children and teenage girls in their *yukata* (summer *kimonos*) are as colourfully dressed as the performers. You find yourself sharing a beer with the carriers of the heavy *mikoshi* (portable shrines). It's times like these that you realise the people behind the exotic masks and costumes are just ordinary citizens, the local bank manager and schoolteacher probably among them, just out celebrating summer or a good harvest.

Finding a local festival isn't as hard as it sounds. Stay in one place long enough and you'll probably be invited to one by your Japanese friends. You might even find yourself dressing up in something you wouldn't normally be seen dead in (like an outfit in the shape of a squid) and walking the streets with the parade. One summer some *gaijin* friends and I constructed our own float and paraded it up and down the main street of our city (during the festival) and though it paled in comparison to the luxurious contraptions our Japanese friends had made, it felt great to be out there and we got plenty of encouraging (and bemused) waves from onlookers during the parade.

There are so many festivals, in fact, particularly in summer, that even just travelling through Japan it's pretty hard not to come across one in full swing, whether it's the Dunjiri festival in Kishiwada,

Osaka, which attracts more than 40,000 spectators every year, or a humble fireworks display in a village of 500 people. To find when and where these festivals are happening, ask your friends and colleagues in your local area.

Play *pachinko*

Like a vertical pinball game, *pachinko* requires gambling away your hard-earned savings under conditions of intense sensory stimulation and is particularly popular among salarymen on their way home from work. To them, it's a way to unwind, although that's hard to believe when you experience *pachinko* for yourself.

The first thing you notice when you enter a *pachinko* parlour for the first time (or any time for that matter) is the sound of millions of ball bearings going around these machines. It hits you like a *tsunami*. It's too loud to talk and your eyes are starting to twitch from the flickering glare of a zillion fluorescent lights. Everywhere you look, down every row of machines in the huge warehouse-sized parlour, people are standing side-by-side like robots feeding their machines with no change of expression or contact between them. After a while (although it may not take that long) you start to feel like an extra in Fritz Lang's *Metropolis*. Either that or you reach sensory overload and leave. Not that it's much better outside with the neon lights flashing out the parlour's name, something like *!!Pachislo!!* or *!!Monaco Palace!!*

If you want to risk your hard earned yen, go to the vending machine just inside the door and buy a basket of balls (¥200 is probably enough for starters, though the regular punters spend up to ¥10,000 at a time). Pick a machine, taking care not to encroach on someone else's (they're like poker machines, people get attached to certain ones). Feed the balls into the slot at the top of the machine and watch them trickle down around the obstacles and into the holes (each of which win you points and thereby more balls) until they're all gone. If you happen to win, take your overflowing tray of ball bearings to the front counter and collect your prize, usually something you don't need, e.g. a cuddly toy, which you then take outside to the 'unofficial' shed in the car park and exchange for cash.

Sing *karaoke*

Karaoke is a much misunderstood and maligned form of entertainment. Unusual, yes, embarrassing at times, certainly, but it's also become one of the most popular forms of entertainment in Japan. While you may find that hard to believe (or perhaps it confirms opinions you already had about the Japanese), it's still worth going to *karaoke* at least once just to see what all the fuss is about. Who knows, you might even like it!

Karaoke (pronounced 'car-ra-oh-kay') literally means 'empty orchestra'. It began in the 1960s as a way of helping would-be professional singers practise their singing in bars and 'snacks' too small to have a live band accompany them.

It's come a long way since then. The songs are now on laser discs, the TV screens can be programmed with songs you want and there are several systems offering foreign songs. The two most popular for foreign *karaoke* stars are: Dam, which has a huge range of classics like Led Zeppelin and David Bowie; and Joy, which tends to have newer releases. When you go to a new *karaoke* place ask to see their English song selection.

Every *gaijin* has a story about the first time they 'did' *karaoke*, so I might as well get mine out of the way. It was when my father visited me in Japan. A group of company executives whom I'd been teaching invited us out for a sumptuous dinner, and when it was time to leave the restaurant they suggested we go to a *karaoke* box. Having never been to *karaoke* before, I was reluctant but feeling there was safety in numbers went along with the idea. No sooner had we settled in to our very own box (looking like a small recording studio) than the managing director of this company, usually a rather quiet, thoughtful man, took the floor with 'My Way', followed by a duet with my dad of 'The Girl from Ipanema'. I waited until everybody had sung before allowing myself to be coerced into choosing a song; managed to find something a bit more up to date, and found that the microphone actually enhanced my voice. 'So that's how they do it!' I thought, and ended up having a great night of unselfconscious fun.

There are two ways to do *karaoke*. *Karaoke* bars are a lot like those embarrassing *karaoke* places back home. They're basically bars and clubs with a TV screen, a microphone and perhaps a small stage. You choose a song from the song book provided, tell someone in charge which song you want, and the words come up on the TV screen against a suitably schmalzy backdrop of a couple walking hand-in-hand along a moonlit beach. In a *karaoke* bar you sing not only in front of your friends but in front of a bunch of people you don't even know (not that most of them will be sober enough to listen anyway).

A more fun (and less embarrassing) option is the *karaoke* box. This is a small room that you and a group of say three or four friends can rent for about ¥2000 per hour (a couple of hours is usually enough). When you go in, a waiter comes to your room to take your order for food and drinks while you look through the song 'menu'. Everyone chooses a song or three they want to sing, and you program the system with the remote control (each song has a reference number). When one of your songs comes up, you take the mike (you can sing sitting down, standing up, whatever) and sing the words from the TV screen. Some of the boxes even have tambourines and drums so you can make your own mix.

A few more 'must do's'

- Soak in an *onsen* (hot spring pool), preferably an outdoor one
- Take part in a tea ceremony
- Catch a peak hour train in Tokyo
- Go on a date with a Japanese girl/boy (it's great for your Japanese!)
- Eat something that looks really suspicious (like sea urchin *sushi*)
- Try on a *kimono* (girls) or *hakama* (those martial arts pants for guys)
- Go to a cherry-blossom viewing party
- Visit a shrine before dawn on New Year's Day (it's freezing!)
- Read a *manga* (a soft-porn comic book)
- Wake up with a *shocchu* hangover.

Leaving

You know you've been in Japan too long when you raise two fingers for the peace sign every time someone points a camera at you. Worse still, you don't even realise you've done it until the photos are developed. It's time to go when you believe compliments about how good your Japanese is or how well you use chopsticks, when you feel overworked if you have to teach more than 25 hours a week, or you feel disappointed if people don't stare at you every time you walk down the street.

In every journey there comes a time to move on. And whether you're leaving Japan or just moving from one place to another, there'll be a few loose ends to tie up. This basically means that everything you did to find work, furniture and accommodation when you arrived has to be reversed. Remember that your most valuable (and therefore most in demand) possessions are your job and your living space. If you've been teaching English, you might also have to find teachers to replace you, particularly if you have private students.

Getting rid of your things is probably easier in Japan than anywhere else. There's always a fresh crew of *gaijin* looking for apartments, transport and furniture to set themselves up. 'What goes around comes around' really is true in Japan. Remember when you were just off the plane and people helped you out? Now it's time to pass some of that goodwill on, so just giving things away can be the least complicated and most generous option.

The Daily Yomiuri places private, non-commercial advertisements in its 'Reader-to-Reader' classifieds every Wednesday for free. The ad can be up to 20 words and the total price of all items listed for sale must be less than ¥100,000. There are five main categories: For Sale, Giveaways (remember, this is Japan), Wanted, Share Accommodation and Personals. You can advertise anything from accommodation to a car, scooter, computer, phone lines or furniture. Fax your ad to Reader-to-Reader Market, *The Daily Yomiuri* on (03) 3217 9847 or mail it to 1-7-1 Otemachi, Chiyoda-ku, Tokyo, 100-8055.

When sending stuff home you can use either mail or, if you've accumulated larger valuables during your stay, international removalists. Mail is the cheapest option. As an example, a 20 kg box sent to Australia or New Zealand will cost ¥27,150 by air mail (which takes about a week), ¥19,550 by SAL (Surface Airlifted, which takes anywhere from a week to a couple of months) and ¥10,250 by sea mail (which takes about three to four months). Three large international removalists are Econoship (call toll free 0120 222111), Excel International (0120 882 110) and Nihon System Service (0120 291 200). Check the English Telephone Directory or the English language newspapers for other companies. As a guideline, Excel International charges ¥47,000 to move one cubic metre of goods from Osaka to Sydney, ¥50,000 to London and ¥45,000 to Los Angeles.

If you want to forward mail from your Japanese address to your home address, you'll need to visit your local post office and get a *tenkyo-todoke* card. Fill in the address and your mail will be forwarded for up to one year after you leave.

At the airport. Some airports have a departure tax, so make sure you have enough yen to pay this before you go through customs and immigration. At Kansai (Osaka) departure tax is ¥2650. At Narita (Tokyo) it's ¥2040 but is included in your air ticket. Since renovations in 1999 Fukuoka Airport now has a Passenger Service Facilities Charge of ¥900 per person for international departures, but again it's included in the price of your air ticket. Nagoya also has a Passenger Service Facilities Charge of ¥750 which is not included in your airfare and must be paid by all departing international passengers.

It's at the airport that you give up your alien status, handing over your Alien Card on your way through immigration. Ironically, your days as an alien are finally over when you least feel like one.

Don't be surprised if you arrive at the airport to see a party of students and friends, some of whom you didn't even know that well. They've come to see you off (sometimes bearing presents and goodbye cards), so things can get quite emotional when it's time for you to step through the doors to the departure lounge. It's just another part of the experience: you haven't left Japan yet! And perhaps they won't be the only ones with tears in their eyes …

Appendix

Books

Working and living in Japan

Best, D., *Make a Mil-Yen – Teaching English in Japan,* Stone Bridge Press, 1994
Brockman, T., *The Job Hunter's Guide to Japan,* Kodansha, Tokyo, 1990
Davidson, R., *Living and Working in Japan,* Yohan Publications, 1992
DeVrye, C., *Japan: An A-Z, A Guide to Living and Working in Japan,* Harper Collins, Sydney, 1994
DuBois, J., S. Gutman, C. Canfield, *Now Hiring! Jobs in Asia,* Perpetual Press, Seattle, 1994
Gaultier, M., *Making it in Japan,* Sanseido, Tokyo, 1993
Gibbs, J.C., *Guide to Jobs in Japan,* Global Village Media Co, 1998
Griffith, S., *Teaching English Abroad,* Vacation Press, Oxford, 1994
Hoopes, A., *How to Live and Work in Japan,* How To Books, Plymouth, 1992
O'Sullivan, J., *Teaching English in Japan,* Passport Books, USA, 1996
March, R., *Working for a Japanese Company,* Kodansha, Tokyo, 1992
Rickman, J., Kusunoki, T., (eds.), *Japan: For Businessman and Job Hunter,* Borgnan, Tokyo, 1993
Rickman, J., *Japan for the Impoverished,* Borgnan, Tokyo, 1995
Wharton, J., *English in Asia,* Global Press, Rockville, 1992
Wharton, J., *Jobs in Japan,* Global Press, Rockville, 1993
Wordell, C., Gorusch, G., *Teach English in Japan,* The Japan Times, 1993

Background reading

Dalby, L., *The Tale of Murasaki,* Doubleday, 2000
Barr, P., *The Deer Cry Pavilion: a story of Westerners in Japan 1868-1905,* Macmillan, Melbourne, 1968
Christopher, R., *The Japanese Mind,* Simon & Schuster, New York, 1983
Clavell, J., *Shogun,* Cornet, any edition
Duffy, J., and Anson, A., (eds.) *Encounters with Japan: 20 Extraordinary Stories,* Angus & Robertson, Pymble, 1994
Japan Culture Institute, *Discover Japan: Words, Customs & Concepts,* (2nd ed) Kodansha, 1987
Kerr, A., *Lost Japan,* Lonely Planet, Melbourne, 1996
Morley, P., *The Mountain is Moving: Japanese Women's Lives,* UBC Press, 1999
Morton, W.S., *Japan: Its History and Culture,* McGraw-Hill, New York, 1984

Raucat, T., *The Honourable Picnic*, Charles Tuttle, Tokyo, 1972
Reischauer, E., *The Japanese*, Belknap Press, Cambridge Mass., 1977
Storry, R., *A History of Modern Japan*, Penguin, Harmondsworth Middlesex, 1976
Yamaguchi, M., Kojima, S., (eds.). *A Cultural Dictionary of Japan*, Japan Times, Tokyo, 1980
Culture Shock! Japan, Times Books International, Singapore, 1993
Yoshikawa, E., *Musashi*, Harper Row/Kodansha, New York, 1981

Travel guides

All the major guidebook publishers—including Lonely Planet, Rough Guides, Insight, Fodor, Frommer, Cadogan and Baedekers—have a guide to Japan. Most major Japanese cities also have city guides.

Phrasebooks

While some teachers claim that phrasebooks can be counterproductive if you're serious about learning a language (the reasoning being it's better to learn the structure of a language than just phrases), phrasebooks do come in handy, particularly when you're new to a country and its language.

Dictionaries

When buying a dictionary, make sure it's English/Japanese and Japanese/English and that the Japanese words are spelt in *romaji* (i.e. using the English alphabet). Electronic dictionaries can be a good investment, particularly if you plan on staying in Japan for a while or studying Japanese. Shop around Akihabara, the electronics district of Tokyo, where prices range from ¥10,000 to ¥25,000.

Textbooks

If you're taking a course, go with whatever your teacher recommends. For self-study, find a text with accompanying cassette tapes; there are lots to choose from including *Japanese for Busy People* published by Kodansha. *Kana Can Be Easy* by Kunihiko Ogawa and published by *The Japan Times* makes learning written Japanese easy by showing how each *katakana* and *hiragana* symbol can be imagined as a picture. Check your nearest foreign language bookshop for others; the main ones are Kinokuniya, Maruzen, Asahiya and Sanseido. Note that Japanese language books produced by Japanese publishers are significantly cheaper in Japan than back home.

The Web

www.majic.co.jp/TELLnet Tokyo English Life Line (TELL) is a community service that provides detailed practical information on everything you need to know about living in Japan. Excellent resource.

www.jpf.go.jp/ Information on the Japan Foundation's activities. Country websites include: www.ozemail.com.au/~jcclib/ (Sydney), www.nihongocentre.org.uk/ (London), www.japanfoundationcanada.org/ (Toronto), www.jfny.org/jfny/index.html (New York) and www.jflalc.org/ (Los Angeles).

www.jnto.go.jp The Japan National Tourist Organisation's comprehensive website, for up-to-date information and tips on travelling in Japan.

www.japantravel.com.au The Japan Travel Bureau's site, offering general information for visitors to Japan.

www.tokyoonthecheap.com Shows how to save money in one of the most expensive cities on earth by listing cheap places to eat, public libraries, free cybercafes, secondhand stores, coupons, even campsites.

www.english.itp.ne.jp English Telephone Directory on the net (the directory is also called Townpage). You can search for listings or browse the info on living, travelling and doing business in Japan.

www.nhk.or.jp/daily Daily national news bulletins in English from NHK.

www.tokyoclassified.com Tokyo Classifieds (jobs, accommodation, general info).

www.kto.co.jp/ *Kansai Time Out*, fantastic monthly magazine catering for foreigners around Osaka/Kobe/Kyoto. Articles, local resources, gig guides, reviews. Everything except the classifieds.

www.tokyo.to/ *Tokyo Journal*, a monthly foreigners' magazine online. Includes up-to-date listings of art, film, music, performing arts, nightlife, eating out and events in Tokyo, as well as employment and accommodation classifieds.

www.japantimes.co.jp/ *The Japan Times* English newspaper online.

www.yomiuri.co.jp/index-e.htm *The Daily Yomiuri* newspaper online.

www.beingabroad.gol.com/ Being Abroad is an online magazine for English-speaking women living and working in Japan. Includes events, chat rooms, resources and classifieds.

www.skijapanguide.com Snow reports, travel guides, feature articles and reservation info for more than 400 ski and snowboard resorts in Japan.

www.outdoorjapan.com Comprehensive guide to Japan's great outdoors. Includes weekly weather updates, festivals, classifieds and chat room.

www.tokyoq.com Tokyo Q is a comprehensive nightlife website.

www.mofa.go.jp/ Ministry of Foreign Affairs, Japan. Includes detailed information on visas, visiting and living in Japan.

Jin.jcic.or.jp/atlas A virtual travel guide to festivals, nature, architecture, street culture, crafts and historic sites with clickable maps.

http://www.yadokari.co.jp/home_E.htm Details on hotels and inns.

Japanese radio, television & movies

Listening to the language, even if you can't understand anything, will give you an appreciation of the sounds and intonation. If your hometown has a sizeable Japanese population, you've got a good chance of finding at least one Japanese radio station. Better still, watch some Japanese TV or films. In Australia, SBS TV broadcasts Japanese news at 5.30 am daily (at least the pictures will give you some idea of meaning).

Japanese films can give you real insight into the culture, as well as the language, before you go. Look out for Japanese Film Festivals in your home city (ask at your local Japan Foundation or check their websites). Some cities have Japanese video stores; Sydney, for example, has Channel 11 in Chatswood, Video Japan in Neutral Bay, and Video-ya in Bondi Junction. Or browse through your video library for classics (with English subtitles) such as Juzo Itami's *Tampopo*, *A Taxing Woman* and *The Funeral*; Oshima Nagisa's *Merry Christmas Mr Lawrence*; *Shogun*; Shohei Imamura's *The Ballad of Nara-yama* and *Black Rain*; any films by Akira Kurosawa; *Seven Samurai* or any of the 23-odd Godzilla movies.

Useful addresses at home

Australia
Embassy of Japan: 112 Empire Circuit, Yarralumla ACT2600. Tel: (02) 6273 3244. www.japan.org.au **Consulate-Generals:** Melbourne Central Tower, 360 Elizabeth Street, Melbourne 3000. Tel: (03) 9639 3244. Colonial Centre, 52 Martin Place, Sydney 2000. Tel: (02) 9231 3455. Comalco Place, 12 Creek Street, Brisbane 4000. Tel: (07) 3221 5188. The Forrest Centre, 221 St George's Terrace, Perth 6000. Tel: (08) 9321 7816. Cairns Corporate Tower, 15 Lake St, Cairns 4870. Tel: (07) 4051 5177. **The Japan Foundation**: 201 Miller Street, North Sydney 2060. Tel: (02) 9957 5322. **Exchange HQ**, 91 York Street, Sydney 2000. Tel: (02) 8235 7090. **Japan National Tourist Organisation:** Level 33, The Chifley Tower, 2 Chifley Square, Sydney 2000. Tel: (02) 9232 4522. **Australia Japan Society**-Sydney, PO Box 218, Willoughby 2068. Tel: (02) 9958 3977. See embassy website for others.

New Zealand
Embassy of Japan: Majestic Centre, 100 Willis Street, Wellington. Tel: (04) 473 1540. www.japan.org.nz **Consulate-Generals:** ASB Bank Centre, 135 Albert Street, Auckland. Tel: (09) 303 4106. Forsyth Barr House, 764 Colombo Street, Christchurch. Tel: (03) 366 5680.

United Kingdom
Embassy of Japan: 101-104 Piccadilly, London W1V 9FN. Tel: (020) 465

6500. www.embjapan.org.uk **Consulate-Generals:** 2 Melville Crescent, Edinburgh EH3 7HW. Tel: (0131) 225 4777. **The Japan Foundation:** 17 Old Park Lane, London W1Y 3LG. Tel: (171) 499 4726. **Japan National Tourist Organisation:** Heathcoat House, 20 Savile Row, London W1X 1AE. Tel: (0171) 734 9638.

Ireland

Embassy of Japan: Nutley Building, Merrion Centre, Nutley Lane, Dublin 4. Tel: (353-1) 269 4244. www.mofa.go.jp/embjapan/ireland/index.htm

Canada

Embassy of Japan: 255 Sussex Drive, Ottawa Ontario K1N 9E6. Tel: (613) 241 8541. www.embassyjapancanada.org **Consulate-Generals:** 900 Board of Trade Tower, 1177 West Hastings Street, Vancouver, BC V6E 2K9. Tel: (604) 684 5868. Edmonton: (780) 422 3752. Toronto: (416) 363 7038. Montréal: (514) 866 3429. **The Japan Foundation:** 131 Floor Street West, Suite 213, Toronto, Ontario M53 1R1. Tel: (416) 966 1600. **Japan National Tourist Organisation:** 165 University Ave, Toronto Ont M5H 3B8. Tel: (416) 366 7140.

United States

Embassy of Japan: 2520 Massachusetts Avenue, N.W., Washington DC 20008-2869. Tel: (202) 238 6700. www.embjapan.org **Main Consulate-Generals:** 299 Park Avenue, New York NY 10171. Tel: (1-212) 371 8222. Atlanta: (404) 892 2700. San Francisco: (415) 777 3533. Chicago: (312) 280 0400. Detroit: (313) 567 0120. Houston: (713) 652 2977. Boston: (617) 973 9772. Honolulu: (808) 543 3111. Los Angeles: (213) 617 6700. **The Japan Foundation**: 152 West 57th Street, New York NY 10019. Tel: (212) 489 0299. The Water Garden, 2425 Olympic Boulevard, Santa Monica CA 90404-4034. Tel: (310) 449 0027. **Japan National Tourist Organisation:** One Rockefeller, Plaza, New York NY 10020. Tel: (212) 757 5640. 401 N. Michigan Ave, Chicago IL 60611. Tel: (312) 222 0874. 515 S. Figueroa St, Los Angeles CA 90071. Tel: (213) 623 1952.

Useful addresses in Japan

For a complete listing of all embassies and consulates, go to the English Telephone Directory at www.english.itp.ne.jp and do a search for 'Embassies and Consulates'.

Australian Embassy: 2-1-14 Mita, Minato-ku, Tokyo 108-8361. Tel: (03) 5232 4111. www.australia.or.jp/english/index.htm

New Zealand Embassy: 20-40 Kamiyama-cho, Shibuya-ku, Tokyo 150-0047. Tel: (03) 3467 2271 www.embassy.kcom.ne.jp/newzealand/index.htm

British Embassy: 1 Ichibancho, Chiyoda-ku, Tokyo. Tel: (03) 3265 5511. www.uknow.or.jp
Embassy of Ireland, Ireland House, 2-10-7 Kojimachi, Chiyoda-ku 102, Tokyo. Tel: (03) 3263-0695. www.embassy.kcom.ne.jp/ireland/index.htm
Embassy of Canada, 7-3-38 Akasaka, Minato-ku, Tokyo. Tel: (03) 5412 6200. www.dfait-maeci.gc.ca/ni-ka/menu-e.asp
US Embassy, 1-10-5 Akasaka, Minato-ku, Tokyo 1107-8420. Tel: (03) 3224 5000. Fax: (03) 3224 5856. http://usembassy.state.gov/japan/

Japan Association for Working Holiday Makers

Tokyo head office: Sunplaza 7F, 4-1-1 Nakano, Nakano-ku, Tokyo 164. Tel: (03) 3389 0181. Fax: (03) 3389 1563. Nearest station is Nakano station on the JR Chuo line (30 minutes from Tokyo station). Open Mon–Sat, closed 5th Sat of every month. **Osaka office:** Osaka-Furitsu Kinro-Seishonen-Kaikan 2F, 2-3-1 Miharadai, Sakai-shi, Osaka 590-01. Tel: (0722) 96 5741. Fax: (0722) 96 5752. Nearest station is Izumigaoka station on the Senboku-Kousoku line (30 minutes from Nanba). Otherwise take a subway from Shin-Osaka station, change at Nakamozu to the Senboku-Kousoku line and it's only 10 minutes from there to Izumigaoka. Open Tues–Sat. **Kyushu office:** Maison Aqua 3F, 1-3-20 Arato, Chuo-ku, Fukuoka-shi, Fukuoka 810-0062. Tel: (092) 713 0854. Fax: (092) 752 2415. Nearest station is Ohorikoen station on the Subway Airport line (10 minutes from Hakata Station). Take the No.2 subway exit. Open Mon–Sat. www.mmjp.or.jp/jawhm/contents.htm

Important telephone numbers in Japan

There are hundreds of services set up to help *gaijin* in Japan. Some of these are listed below and most, if not all, have English speaking operators. If someone answers in Japanese, say '*Eigo ga dekimasu ka*' ('Can you speak English?'). The person will then usually switch to English or transfer you to an English speaker.

Emergency telephone numbers

These are free calls if using a public phone—just press the red button before dialling. Police: 110. Fire and ambulance: 119. To report a fire say '*Kaji desu*' ('There's a fire') and for medical emergencies say '*Kyukyu desu*' ('First Aid'). In either case you'll have to give your name and address, so it's a good idea to practise saying these in Japanese. The Japan HelpLine: 0120 461 997. Directory Assistance: 104 (for numbers in Japan) and 0057 (for numbers in other countries). The English Telephone Directory website (english.itp.ne.jp) lists all emergency phone numbers as well as phone numbers of hospitals, airports, lost and found and information services for foreigners.

Daily living information services

Every major city in Japan has an international centre and many have additional services for foreigners. Following are the main advisory centres for foreigners.

Japan Hotline, Tokyo: (03) 3586 0110. Yokohama Information Corner: (045) 671 7209. Nagoya International Centre, Information Counter: (052) 581 0100. Sapporo International Plaza: (011) 211 2105. Sendai International Centre, International Exchange & Information Area: (022) 265 2471. Sendai English Hotline: (022) 224 1919. Osaka International House, Information Centre: (06) 6773 8989. Osaka Prefectural Information Service for Foreign Residents: (06) 6941 2297. Kobe International Community Centre: (078) 291 8441. Kobe International Plaza: (078) 795 4400. Kyoto International Community House: (075) 752 3511. Centre for Multicultural Information and Assistance, Kyoto: (075) 604 5625. Nara International Foundation: (0742) 27 2436. Hiroshima International Centre: (082) 541 3888. Rainbow Plaza, Fukuoka: (092) 733 2220. Nagasaki International Association: (095) 823 3931. Okayama Prefectural International Exchange Foundation: (086) 256 2000.

Foreigners' information and counselling services

Tokyo English Life Line (TELL) is a non-profit community service organisation that provides information, support and counselling to the international community in Japan. TELL offers a free counselling service and is open 9 am–4 pm and 7 pm–11 pm daily. Tel: (03) 3968 4099. TELL Community Counselling Service provides face-to-face counselling; for an appointment phone (03) 5721 4455.

Japan Help Line is a 24 hour emergency service: (0120) 461 997. The HIV/AIDS Hotline is a 24-hour, multilingual free service: (0120) 461 955. Alcoholics Anonymous Japan, General Service Office (in Tokyo) is on (03) 3590 5377.

The English Help Line will translate for you in an emergency or help if you get lost. Tel: (03) 5320 7744. The JR English Info Line will help with JR's transport services throughout Japan; for Tokyo call (03) 3423-0111. For any queries regarding NTT (telephone) services, call (012) 364463 toll free.

International exchange associations

Just about every city or ward has an international exchange association. These provide free information and advice on anything to do with living in Japan, from how to read a Japanese train timetable, to how to pay your phone bill and where to buy shoes in larger sizes. For the phone number of your local association, ask at your city office for *Kokusai Koryu Kyokai no denwa bango o oshiete kudasai*.

Japanese immigration information centres

Contact the Immigration Control Bureau in your city for information on visas and re-entry permits. Tokyo: (03) 3213 8523. Osaka: (06) 6774 3413. Nagoya: (052) 951 2391. Yokohama: (045) 661 5110 or 211 0365. Japanese Consulate in Pusan, Korea: (8251) 465 5101. Japanese Consulate in Hong Kong: (852) 2522 1184.

Useful phrases

Remember to pronounce every syllable equally and make your intonation rather flat. An exception is 'u' at the end of a word (e.g. 'desu') because it's usually silent. The letter 'r' is pronounced as if it is halfway between 'l' and 'r' so that it almost sounds like a 'd'. Pronunciation is straightforward and unlike in English doesn't vary with the word. In all words the basic vowels are pronounced as follows: 'a' as in car; 'i' as in lip; 'u' as in blue; 'e' as in egg; 'o' as in hot.

Just a minute/wait a minute *chotto matte kudasai*
Help! *Tasukete!*

Communicating

Can you speak English? – *eigo ga dekimasu ka*
I don't speak Japanese – *nihongo o hanashimasen*
Do you understand? – *wakarimasu ka*
I don't understand – *wakarimasen*

Asking for help

Can you help me, please? (casual) – *chotto ii desu ka*
Would you take a photo (of me/us)? – *shashin o totte moraemasu ka*
Do you mind if I take a photo? – *shashin o tottemo ii desu ka*
Where? – *doko*
When? – *itsu*
What? – *nani*
Why? – *nan de* or *doshite*
Who? – *dare* or *donata*
How much? – *ikura*

Asking for directions

Where is the ...? – *... wa doko desu ka*
Toilet – *toire/benjo*
Tourist office – *kanko anaijo*
Bank – *ginko*
I understand – *wakarimasu*
What does that mean? – *doyu imi desu ka*
How do you say that in Japanese? – *sore wa nihongo de nan to iimasu ka*
Look out! – *Abunai!*
Currency exchange office – *ryogaejo*
Post office – *yubinkyoku*
Police box – *koban*
Police – *keisatsu*
Train station – *eki*
Subway station – *chikatetsu no eki*
Ticket office – *kippu uriba*
Bus stop – *basu tei*
Right – *migi*
Left – *hidari*
Straight ahead – *masugu*
Near – *chikai*
Far – *toi*

Some travel phrases

Does this train (bus) go to ... ? –

Kono densha (basu) wa ... ni ikimasu ka

Where can I get a ticket for ... ? – *... yuki no kippu wa doko de kaemasu ka*

How much is it to ... ? – *... made wa ikura desu ka*

Would you let me know when the train/bus gets to ... ? – *... ni tsui tara oshiete kudasai*

The bill, please – *chekku purizu*

Greetings

Good morning (before about 10 am) – *o hayo gozaimasu*

Hello (throughout the day until evening) – *konnichiwa*

Good evening (after dark) – *konbanwa*

Goodbye – *sayonara* or bye bye!

See you later (more casual than goodbye) – *mata ne* or *ja mata*

Take care – *ki o tsukete*

Good night – *oyasumi nasai*

My name is ... – *watashi no namae wa (your name) desu*

I'm (name) ... – *watashi wa (your name) desu*

Nice to meet you – *hajime mashite*

How are you? (usually said only when you haven't seen the person for a while) – *o genki desu ka*

Fine, thank you – *genki desu*

And you? – *anata wa*

Basic phrases and words

Thank you (very much) – *arigato (gozaimasu)*

Thanks – *domo*

You're welcome – *do itashi mashite*

Yes – *hai*

No – *iie*

Excuse me – *sumi masen*

Sorry – *gomen nasai*

Please (when asking for something) – *onegai shimasu*

Please (when offering something) – *dozo*

Foreigner – *gaijin* or *gaikokujin*

Japanese person – *nihon-jin*

Australian – *osutoraria-jin*

New Zealander – *nyujirando-jin*

English person – *igirisu-jin*

Irish person – *airurando-jin*

American – *amerika-jin*

Canadian – *kanada-jin*

English language – *eigo*

Japanese language – *nihongo*

Me – *watashi*

You – *anata*

We/us – *watashi-tachi*

Her – *kanojo*

Him – *kare*

Time phrases

What time is it? – *ima nan-ji desu ka*

It's ... o'clock – *... -ji desu*

Now – *ima*

Later – *ato de*

Today – *kyo*

Tomorrow – *ashita*

Yesterday – *kino*

The day before yesterday – *ototoi*

The day after tomorrow – *asatte*

Morning – *asa*

Afternoon – *gogo*

Evening – *yugata*

Night – *yoru*

Sunday – *nichi-yobi*

Monday – *getsu-yobi*

Tuesday – *ka-yobi*

Wednesday – *sui-yobi*

Thursday – *moku-yobi*

Friday – *kin-yobi*

Saturday – *do-yobi*

January – *ichi-gatsu*

February – *ni-gatsu*

March – *san-gatsu*

April – *shi-gatsu*
May – *go-gatsu*
June – *roku-gatsu*
July – *shichi-gatsu*
August – *hachi-gatsu*
September – *ku-gatsu*
October – *ju-gatsu*
November – *juichi-gatsu*
December – *juni-gatsu*

Numbers

0	zero	1	ichi
2	ni	3	san
4	yon/shi	5	go
6	roku	7	nana/shichi
8	hachi	9	kyu
10	ju	11	ju-ichi
12	ju-ni	13	ju-san
14	ju-yon	15	ju-go
16	ju-roku	17	ju-nana/ju-shichi
18	ju-hachi	19	ju-kyu
20	ni-ju	21	ni-ju-ichi
30	san-ju	100	hyaku
200	ni-hyaku	1000	sen
2000	ni-sen	5000	go-sen
10,000	ichi-man	20,000	ni-man

30,000	san-man
100,000	ju-man
1,000,000	hyaku-man
100,000,000	ichi-oku

Counters (for counting objects)

one	hitotsu	two	futatsu
three	mittsu	four	yottsu
five	itsutsu	six	muttsu
seven	nanatsu	eight	yattsu
nine	kokonotsu	ten	to

Coins

Every coin and note is yen and is pronounced 'en'.

¥1	=	*ichi-en* (one yen)
¥5	=	*go-en*
¥10	=	*ju-en*
¥50	=	*go-ju-en*
¥100	=	*hyaku-en*
¥500	=	*go-hyaku-en*

Notes

¥1000	=	*sen-en*
¥2000		*ni-sen-en*
¥5000	=	*go-sen-en*
¥10,000	=	*ichi-man-en*

In Japanese 10,000 is referred to as a '*man*' (pronounced 'marn'). 10,000 is *ichi-man* (literally 'one-*man*'); 20,000 is *ni-man*, and so on. Don't say ten-thousand or *ju-sen*, there's no such thing. Similarly 100,000 is *ju-man* (or ten-ten thousands).

Notes:

Notes: